MW00989987

Great
RoadRides
Denver

Jay P. K. Kenney

FULCRUM
GOLDEN, COLORADO

The information in *Great Road Rides Denver*
is accurate as of May 2010. However, if something in the book is incorrect, please write
to the author in care of Fulcrum Publishing,
4690 Table Mountain Drive, Suite 100, Golden,
Colorado 80403; fulcrum@fulcrumbooks.com.

Great Road Rides Denver provides many safety
tips, but good decision making and sound
judgment are the responsibility of the individual. Neither the publisher nor the author
assumes any liability for injury that may arise
from the use of this book.

Library of Congress Cataloging-in-
Publication Data

Kenney, Jay P. K.
  Great road rides Denver / Jay P. K. Kenney.
    p. cm.
  Includes bibliographical references and index.
  ISBN 978-1-55591-737-1 (pbk.)
  1. Cycling--Colorado--Denver--Guidebooks.
2. Bicycle
trails--Colorado--Denver--Guidebooks. 3.
Bicycle
lanes--Colorado--Denver--Guidebooks. 4.
Denver (Colo.)--Guidebooks. I.
Title.
  GV1045.5.C62K46 2010
  796.60978883--dc22

                          2010009238

Printed on recycled paper in the United States
by Malloy Inc.
0 9 8 7 6 5 4 3 2 1

Design by Jack Lenzo
Cover: Bike photo © Jack Lenzo
Denver skyline © Shutterstock | Rebecca
Dickerson

Fulcrum Publishing
4690 Table Mountain Drive, Suite 100
Golden, Colorado 80403
800-992-2908 • 303-277-1623
www.fulcrumbooks.com

For Emily first,
then Clayton, Duncan, Ben,
and Izzy. The rest of my family—
sine quibus non.

Never let the fear of being lost
interfere with the enjoyment of
not knowing where you are.
—Anonymous

Contents

Most people tend to be creatures of habit when it comes to cycling. They find a couple of routes they like and ride them routinely and regularly. In metro Denver, those routes usually involve the Cherry Creek Trail, the Platte River Trail, or some variant of the two. These routes have some advantages: they are predictable, relatively free from cars, and accessible. But using them exclusively means that you miss out on some of the best riding the greater Denver area has to offer, rides that take you from Arvada to Centennial, from Golden to Commerce City. If you stay on the trails your whole cycling life, you will miss out on these and other rides. You will also miss out on the pulse and culture of the city: the urban hipness of the Highlands, the Latino influence on the east and west sides, the gritty industrialism up north, and the benign suburbanism of the south and east. Only by taking to the streets and exploring the city will you begin to appreciate what a wealth of great cycling Denver has to offer.

The idea for this book came about in 2007 when gasoline prices hovered near $4 a gallon, and many, like me, were avoiding "drive to ride" routes in order to lessen their pain at the pump. In addition to enjoying the extra cash, I have always been a restless cyclist, eager to explore new territory, willing to get lost in the process, and happy to spend a few extra minutes finding my way around or through a particularly difficult intersection. I believed you should be able to get on your bike anywhere in the metro area and ride interesting routes of varying lengths without first getting into your car and driving someplace else. Not that there aren't great rides accessible by car. I love riding Deer Creek Canyon, Squaw Pass, Golden Gate Canyon, and the high passes in Colorado's mountains, but I cannot do that every day from my house in Denver. And that's what I wanted: a variety of rides of varying length, difficulty, and interest, all accessible from metro Denver. I wasn't averse to using the major trail systems, but I wanted to go beyond them, to see more of this burgeoning city that I've known in one way or another for almost 40 years.

But first things first. If you are new to cycling or to Denver, get yourself oriented to the trail systems. Surely one of them is close by: either Cherry Creek, South Platte River, Clear Creek, or Bear Creek. These trails, of which Denver and the surrounding cities are justly proud, are a great introduction to metro cycling and an easy way to get around the city by bike. But don't stop there. Get off the trails and onto the streets. Explore. The routes in this book take advantage of the many streets that are perfect for cycling. The speed limits are low, the traffic friendly, and/or the roads wide and marked for cyclists. There are miles and miles of streets like this in the city, and once you try them out for yourself, you'll never be content exclusively riding the bike trails again. There's just too much to see, whether it be the incredible number of parks and golf courses that dot the area or the amazing variety of architectural styles to be found in the various neighborhoods.

Another advantage of taking to the streets is encountering varied terrain. Most of the trail systems follow main drainages, and the trails are relatively flat and do not climb or fall more than 10 to 20 feet per mile. Contrast that with the climb up Dartmouth Avenue west to Loretto Heights, or the hills on Zuni Street, where the grade varies from 5 percent to almost 10 percent.

The routes in this guide are scattered throughout the city but are organized alphabetically. I have ridden and mapped each one multiple times. They range in length from 17 to 65 miles and climb as much as 5,000 feet and as little as 200 feet (although the measurements of distance and elevation gain are averages and your cycling computer may produce slightly different figures). Five supplemental maps are included. They provide much-needed detail for a few troublesome and complex areas. There is also a map showing the major trail systems in the metro area.

Each route description includes basic information about the route as well as information to help you decide if it is the right route for you. You will be able to see at a glance how much or little of the route is on the streets as opposed to being on a trail or in a park. You can also see how difficult, in my estimation, the route finding is, and you can tell if the traffic is likely to be light or heavy and where any particularly difficult spots are. Finally, I suggest a direction to take, whether clockwise or counterclockwise, which corresponds to the directions in the text, though for many routes either way works fine.

If you are new to Denver cycling, familiarize yourself with the shorter routes first. They have more detailed information than the longer routes, all of which build upon the legs of the shorter routes. The longer routes usually assume some familiarity with the earlier stages of the ride as you leave and return to central Denver.

I have included a recommended starting place for each ride and a direction, but you should try nearly every ride in both directions. Riding an old route in a new direction is like riding a new route altogether.

Most of the routes start or pass by the intersection of Downing Street and Speer Boulevard. But if you live somewhere far from this landmark, don't despair; it's just a landmark and an organizational tool. Most of the routes in the book are loops, so pick up the route you want wherever it's convenient for you to do so and ride it as far as you want. More important, make up your own routes and variations, and link the routes listed in this guide to make new ones. Presented here are just some of my top choices. More are yet to be explored, particularly in Arvada, Littleton, Adams County, and Aurora.

When you first head out on a new route, take a copy of the map with you. It will likely take you longer to ride a new route the first time, and you may go slightly awry. But don't let these things bother you. They are half the fun of a new ride. Stop and look around. Ask strangers and other cyclists for directions. It helps to keep the basic grid structure of the city in your head. Broadway divides east from west, and Ellsworth Avenue north from south. Forty and 65 blocks east of Broadway puts you on Colorado and Monaco boulevards, repectively. Twenty-one and 31 blocks south of Ellsworth are Evans and Hampden avenues, while 36 and 92 blocks west of Broadway are Lowell and Garrison streets. Streets and boulevards run north and south, avenues east and west. One mile equals approximately 9 blocks north and south, and 15 blocks east and west. The foothills and mountains are west. It is generally a downhill ride from south to north (the direction in which the South Platte River flows) and uphill whenever you leave the Platte River Valley (west to the foothills and east to the plains).

As you plan your ride, you should consider what to take along. I never leave home without an extra inner tube, an air supply in the form of carbon dioxide cartridges and an inflator, a small patch kit, tire levers, two Allen wrenches, and at least one water bottle. I carry my phone in my jersey, inside a plastic bag to keep it dry. For longer rides or in uncertain weather, I add a lightweight rain jacket, arm warmers, a hat, and a snack. I always wear a helmet. Many people ride with music, but I find it distracting and dangerous, since you cannot hear someone approaching from behind.

Although you could spend most of your cycling life on the trails in Denver, the core of this guide requires you to ride on the streets. Intimidating, perhaps, at first, urban cycling allows you to explore the city to a degree impossible in a car or from the trails alone. To help you get started, I've included some thoughts in the author's note on how to ride safely and assertively in traffic. But by traffic, I don't mean the heavy traffic you'll find on Colorado Boulevard or Broadway. Urban riding as defined in this guidebook is on relatively wide streets with light to moderate traffic traveling at slower speeds most of the time. Riding in anything else is just not very much fun.

By getting out onto the streets, you'll make riding safer for yourself and the thousands of other cyclists in the area. The more cyclists who ride on the streets, the safer it is for all, because drivers then become accustomed to the presence, speed, habits, and (sometimes) unpredictability of people on bikes.

Now, get out there and have fun!

Taking to the Streets
Cycling in an Urban Environment

It won't take long to realize that most of the rides in this book have some component of street riding in them. That is, in order to complete the ride or at least have the most fun, you'll have to be comfortable riding on city streets. For some, the transition from dedicated trail riding to taking to the streets may be uncomfortable and provoke anxiety. Riding on the streets, much less in urban traffic, certainly brings out our worst fears, sometimes simply because it's so foreign to us but also because in comparison to a driver in a car, we as cyclists feel small and weak.

Whole books have been written about the psychology of traffic and cycling in an urban environment, the best of which are *Traffic*[1] and *The 'Art of Cycling*,[2] and I encourage you to read them if you're interested in delving further into the matter. In the meantime, there's no substitute for practice and experience. So go out on a Sunday or early in the morning and ride the streets when few drivers are around. If you are a neophyte, head out to the Heather Gardens extension of the Cherry Creek Reservoir Loop. You can warm up on the Cherry Creek Trail, then get your feet wet on a short (3-mile) loop around a retirement community. After that, start linking up the major trail systems and parks, most of which can be joined together without too much time on the roads. Then switch to Saturdays. Try out some of the quieter routes and neighborhoods first. Ride the Central Parks Trifecta and the Stapleton Loop. Look for wide, quiet streets such as Montview Boulevard, 26th Avenue, Dartmouth Avenue, and Irving Street. Ride with a friend and get used to relying on each other to watch out for traffic and the unexpected. In short, start small and work your way up to some of the more urbanized rides: out to Golden on 26th and 20th avenues or out to Cherry Creek Reservoir on the Anti-Trail Loop after work. Most important, know that these routes are designed to take advantage of the best streets in Denver for urban cycling.

Our rights and obligations as cyclists were recently updated and clarified in Colorado. Under state law, bicycles are defined as vehicles and are subject to most of the same statutes and local ordinances as automobiles.[3] The state traffic code, however, bears little resemblance to the way people actually cycle. That is, although cyclists everywhere are subject to the same prohibitions against running red lights and stop signs as are drivers of cars, in practice, enforcement is minimal unless the violation is egregious or there's been an accident. The recent amendments have brought state law and real world cycling slightly closer together, while expanding our rights significantly. Under Colorado's former framework, cyclists were required to ride as close to the right side of the road as possible, were forbidden to ride two abreast, and had no enforceable safe space around them into which automobiles were forbidden to intrude. Under the new law, which took effect on August 7, 2009, cyclists must only ride far enough on the right to help vehicles pass them.[4] How far right is far enough depends on two seemingly simple principles: the right-hand lane must be wide enough to be shared *safely* with overtaking vehicles, and the cyclist may use her own independent (but not unreasonable) judgment to determine how far right she should allow herself to drift. The cyclist's subjective state of mind largely determines what is or is not safe. Under the new legislation, cyclists may consider "hazards at the edge of a roadway, including but not limited to fixed or moving objects, parked or moving vehicles, bicycles, pedestrians, animals, surface hazards, or narrow lanes."[5] I take this to mean that we as cyclists are finally liberated from clinging to the edge of a road. If there are pedestrians, bicycles, animals, narrow lanes, or just junk in the road, we are completely within our legal rights to move left to avoid these obstacles. The other parts of the new bill are less interesting but still useful. For example, drivers can't drive too close to cyclists or drive "in a threatening manner toward or near a bicyclist." A 3-foot margin is explicitly required. Cyclists may ride two abreast if they aren't obstructing traffic. Drivers cannot throw objects at or otherwise taunt bicyclists. And drivers may cross a yellow line in order to pass cyclists safely.[6]

The legislation is a step in the right direction, at least to the extent that it begins to recognize the split between traffic law and cycling practice, and to recognize that cyclists need real protection while riding in traffic. However, there's still work to be done. Watch the flow of bicycle and auto traffic sometime on any of Denver's major streets. Pick Broadway or Colfax, for example. You'll see cyclists riding with and against traffic, on both sidewalks in both directions, and riding with complete disregard for both the regulatory framework and their own safety. Given the freedom and flexibility that bicycles give us, together with an absence of serious traffic enforcement against cyclists, this is probably not surprising. Be aware, however, that our flexibility, freedom, and the absence of traffic enforcement against cyclists absolutely enrage a small minority of drivers. Protect yourself from potentially hazardous auto-cycle confrontations. What plays out in these interactions is largely about power: cyclists have none, drivers have it all, and legal rights are a poor substitute for physical well-being. Being right or having the legal right-of-way will not and does not guarantee your safety; you alone are responsible for your safety when on your bicycle. I watched a cyclist yell and berate a befuddled driver one day at Cherry Creek Reservoir for beginning to turn in front of her. The cyclist certainly had the right-of-way, and her anger and surprise were understandable, but being right would not have kept her out of the hospital if the driver had knocked her over. In an auto-cycle collision, the cyclist will always lose. This is just a matter of simple physics. Whether or not you have the legal right-of-way, if a driver cannot see you (or does not see you), he cannot avoid you.

Understand where the dangers are when you're out cycling the streets. I am convinced that the most dangerous place to ride a bicycle is against traffic on a sidewalk of a major street.[7] Drivers are not looking for you. In their eyes you have appeared unexpectedly. Cyclists travel considerably faster than pedestrians. Drivers are accustomed to the regularity, speed, and frequency of pedestrians, and a cyclist moving even at 7 mph upsets that training and equilibrium. At every curb cut, there is the possibility of a bad auto-cycle interaction.

The second most dangerous place to be on a bicycle is at an intersection where cyclists naturally succumb to two problematic practices: we treat red lights like four-way stops and stop signs like yield signs. Here two dangerous scenarios play out regularly: drivers turn in front of cyclists from the left and cars enter the street cyclists are riding on from the right. In the first scenario, the penalty to cyclists is particularly severe, because there's a likelihood of higher speeds during a vehicle-vehicle collision. The second scenario becomes risky when a driver does not see a cyclist. Remember, drivers are accustomed to seeing other cars, not a small cyclist moving at 15 mph. That intersections are dangerous should not surprise us. They are crash magnets. Fifty percent of all auto crashes occur at intersections. At a four-way intersection, there are 56 potential points of what engineers call "conflict," or the chance for you to run into someone else. Thirty-two of these are places where vehicles can hit other vehicles, including bicycles.[8] Pay attention the next time you see a car entering the street you're traveling on. Standard operating procedure for most drivers is to make an initial stop well beyond the stop line and deep into the pedestrian crosswalk, if there is one, then glance right and left before moving on. That is, drivers automatically intrude at least into the crosswalk if not into your previously safe lane of travel before coming to a stop and looking for oncoming traffic. More often than not, the driver never comes to a complete stop. Cyclists must account for this behavior when riding in traffic and must be able to interpret and react to the ambiguity of the rolling stop. If the driver does not see you when he glances to the left, will you be able to stop or move in time to avoid an accident?

Fortunately, most auto-bicycle interactions are benign, and cyclists' mobility and rapid stopping power gives them a key advantage when unexpectedly confronted with an errant driver. And since the sidewalk is a dangerous place for a cyclist, it is easy enough to stay off it in the first place. When you must use a sidewalk to go a short distance from point A to B (and there are places where you must in Denver), be ever mindful that nobody—not pedestrians, not drivers—expects you to be there. Curiously, in most of Denver, riding on the sidewalk is illegal.[9] As for the rest of our experience on the streets, there's much we can do to make urban cycling experience very safe.

Consider first what Robert Hurst, a longtime Denver bike messenger, calls traffic intensity. Traffic intensity matters a lot to our safety at intersections and elsewhere. In Hurst's mind, traffic intensity is a "function of volume, speed, frequency of turning/crossing vehicles, lane width, and a certain frantic disposition."[10] And, I would add, posted speed limits. Traffic intensity varies with the time of day and day of the week. Even a wide shoulder on I-70 between Genessee and Evergreen Parkway does little to compensate for the venturi effect created when a large tractor-trailer combination whizzes by you at 65 mph. When you're planning your next (or first) ride out on the streets, stop a moment and consider what the intensity of the traffic will likely be. Is it rush hour? Will you be going with the rush-hour traffic (not much fun) or against it (more fun)? What day of the week is it? What time of day is it? In most parts of the metro area, traffic intensity is highest on weekdays and lowest on the weekends. But Saturdays near any of the major malls or shopping centers are likely to be a struggle. Early morning, especially in the hot summer, is a great time to ride, as is almost all day on Sunday any time of year. On some routes you're likely to encounter traffic on every day of the week at almost any time of day. Most of the routes in this guide are designed to avoid streets with significant traffic intensity, and I've noted times when you may want to avoid a route if possible.

You should also factor into your thinking and decision making the kind of street on which you're going to be riding. Is it wide enough for a car to pass you safely within the shared lane? What about a big truck? Does the street have a dedicated bike lane, or shared space? Does it have two lanes in each direction, or one with a middle turning lane? What's the speed limit? Most of the riding described here takes place on streets with low traffic intensity and speed limits less than 35 mph. All these factors or their absence can make your ride safer or require slightly more vigilance on your part. Curiously, *Traffic* cites some studies that suggest that a dedicated bike lane is not necessarily safer than a similarly wide street with a shared-use arrow.[11] One explanation for this paradox is that if you give drivers a painted line between the cyclist and themselves, they assume the line is a hard one and that the cyclist will not cross it but that they can come right up to it. Without a hard line, drivers may be more cautious about giving a cyclist enough room. That said, there are miles of wide streets in the Denver area on which to ride.

But beyond the objective factors involved in safer urban cycling, cycling is an intricate and delicate act of communication between you and traffic. You must communicate both directly and indirectly with the drivers around you to ride gracefully and safely with them. In this regard, it may be helpful to think of traffic as a herd of cattle: they are not very smart, they like to follow each other and stick together, they are easily startled, and there are usually a few unpredictable bulls unexpectedly mixed in with the cows, steers, and heifers. Although you must avoid getting run over at all costs, your job as a cyclist is to ride quietly next to the herd. At times you may need to direct the cattle in a safe loop around you, but you must not startle any individual unnecessarily, and avoid direct confrontations with bulls.

Cyclists communicate with drivers in many ways, directly and indirectly. A child on a bike with training wheels wobbling down the street communicates inexperience and scares most drivers into giving the child a very wide berth; where one driver swings wide, so, often, will any following drivers. A young male on a road bike in full racing kit with a matching helmet may likely communicate a level of competence such that drivers will give him less room than he may want or expect. Your ability to glance over your outside shoulder to check for oncoming traffic behind you may communicate both competence (if you don't deviate from your line unnecessarily) and a wish to move into the lane next to you. Your direct communications with your hands or your head to show your direction, or to indicate where you want a particular driver to go, are also essential skills in traffic. You can also talk directly to drivers, unnerving as it may be to them. If I'm waiting on a red light in a lane that allows both straight-through and right-turning traffic and there's traffic behind me, I'll frequently turn and ask the driver if he wants to pull up next to me and make a right-hand turn.

Dealing with ambiguous communication is part of the cycling experience. Is the car rolling slowly through the stop sign going to stop when the driver sees you? How can you be sure you've been seen and understood? When the windows are tinted and the glare is strong, the driver may be gesturing and nodding vigorously, but how can you be certain? Is the driver looking in your direction but not seeing you? Is he nodding his head to a phone conversation he's having and not to you? Does he have his head tucked in that giveaway position that says, "I have a cell phone but not a hands-free kit"? The more conservative you are about these kinds of interactions, the safer you will be. These are perfect moments to come to a full stop at the intersection and wait for clarity.

One of the great ways to communicate with the drivers around you is by lane positioning, an underrated but fabulous tool. Start with an obvious application. If you believe it's safe for a driver to pass you within the lane, your position close to the right edge of the lane will indicate that. If you believe it's not safe, your position out toward the middle of the lane should clearly communicate "Don't Pass!" Don't rely on drivers to judge the width of their car, the width of the lane, and how much room you, the cyclist, need. They're bound to get it wrong.

Here's an example involving the much-hated door zone, that area 3 to 5 feet to the side of a parked car into which car doors are unexpectedly opened. Doors hurt when they hit you and hurt worse when you hit them! Scan ahead. If you see a line of parked cars in your future, position yourself appropriately within your lane earlier rather than later, so that when you come up on the cars you'll already be 3 to 4 feet to the left of the doors. In a similar vein, a cyclist hugging the right-hand curb communicates that it's okay for moving cars to drift within 3 to 4 feet of him or her. Drivers prize predictability— if you're hugging the right curb, then suddenly bank left to skirt a line of parked cars, the drivers behind you are likely to be startled by the sudden change. Avoid startling drivers. Most don't react very well to it.

If you're concerned that drivers entering the road from your right may not see you, position yourself well to the left-center of the lane. This is especially true in parts of the city that are overgrown with trees (and therefore frequently in the shade) or where parked cars may obscure your pitiful little cycling self. You may think you're riding safely by staying far right in such situations, but the farther right you ride, the *less* likely it is that a casual driver who glances your way is going to see you. The real danger is from front-left and front-right of you, not behind you. If you anticipate danger from the front, actively move to the place where you have the highest likelihood of being seen. Move to the center of the lane and stay there, at least until you're out of the danger zone.

A variation on this theme happens whenever you ride fast enough to match or exceed the speed of the cars with which you're sharing the road. When you're traveling the speed limit or exceeding it, move and stay near the center of the lane. At 25 to 30 mph, you need to be near the center, both to see and to be seen by drivers entering your lane from either left or right, and to give yourself time to avoid any driver who doesn't see you. The faster you go, the larger the buffer zone in time and distance you need.

Another instance where lane positioning matters and communicates your presence on the road is when you enter an intersection behind one or more cars.

At that particular moment, you're nearly invisible and particularly vulnerable to drivers moving in the opposite direction who are waiting to turn left across your path of travel. If they cannot see you, and only see the cars in front of you and no cars close behind, they may wrongly assume they can shoot the gap behind the car in front of you to make their left turn. If you're positioned near the right rear of the car in front of you, you're likely invisible to the about-to-turn car. You must make yourself visible by moving to the left edge of the lane and standing up in your pedals.

Learning how to handle red lights and stop signs is a critical piece of safe urban cycling. Let's be clear here that the law requires you, the cyclist, to obey stop signs, four-way stops, and red lights just as if you were in a motor vehicle. Noted. But really what cyclists are up against is a choice between safety, efficiency, and legality, and sometimes you can only have two out of three.[12] If you wish to be safe and legal, you stay on the small side streets with little traffic and multiple stop signs and four-way stops that require you to make a full stop every block or so.

Add to this the problem of traffic lights that don't detect the presence of bicycles at a light. In such a case, you can wait all day or until a car shows up to rescue you. The problem lies under your wheels, where an induction coil is supposed to sense the presence of enough metal to trip a switch and initiate a change of lights. Even most steel bikes don't have enough surface area to trip the sensors, much less a full carbon bike. Colorado and Denver both expressly allow you to treat an inoperative traffic light as a stop sign if it remains red "during several time cycles."[13] Here's what common sense teaches. Approach every controlled intersection with care and at a speed slow enough to allow you to stop, if you need to. Yield the right-of-way to all pedestrians and to any other vehicles there before you. If the intersection is clear, proceed on through it, if you can do so safely. At red lights, which often indicate a major intersection, use even more caution. The worst thing you can do at a controlled intersection is to steal the right-of-way from another who has

it legitimately. Our feeling of freedom and concern for efficiency should never outweigh our obligations to others. *Never take the right-of-way from another motorist or cyclist.* Right-of-way theft is just plain wrong and accounts for a significant amount of the hostility to which cyclists are subjected. It's not yours to take. It's for others to give.

A related issue comes up when you come to an intersection and there's a line of cars waiting for the light to change. Should you filter through the cars, move to the head of the line, and then jump the light? Or just wait? Whether to filter through to the front of a line depends upon context and timing. Assuming you have time and there's room to keep you from getting squeezed against a curb, the reasons to do it are clear. Starting up is a cyclist's most vulnerable moment. Our feet are out of the pedals and we're struggling to get clipped in. We have no gyroscopic balance. We're watching for traffic, pedaling for speed, checking our gear by looking down and back, and perhaps putting the water bottle away. Moving to the front allows us to jump out, to get slightly ahead of traffic at the most vulnerable moment, and to create some space around us. But timing is everything. Move to the front only when you're certain you have time to get there. Being trapped at slow speed between a line of cars and the curb is a bad experience.

The most compelling reason to be at the front is so oncoming turning traffic can see you. Consider this: a Chevrolet Suburban is more than 6 feet tall and 7 feet wide. While you're seated on your road bike, the top of your helmet hovers around 5 feet off the ground, and you present a side-to-side profile of about 30 inches. You cannot see cars waiting to turn behind the SUV in front of you, and they cannot see you, even ignoring moderately tinted windows. It's as if you were invisible, riding behind a 40-square-foot wall that opens to reveal you only at the last moment. It's just not a fair contest. The blind spot especially matters when a gap develops in front of you as the light is turning from green to yellow. That puts more pressure on drivers to clear the intersection by turning left across your path. If they only see the gap and cannot see you, the result will be bad for both of you. Moving to the front of the lane avoids this. But if that's not possible, either because there's no room or the timing is wrong (e.g., the light is just turning as you arrive), do this: move to the left side of traffic and stand up as you cross the intersection. That will put you at the highest point of visibility in relation to oncoming cars. Drivers will be able to see you; you will be able to see them. As you can see, cycling in an urban environment is a delicate dance between you and the cars around you.

For all the seriousness of the tone here, don't forget that cycling comes with its own special joie de vivre. On the routes laid out in this book, you'll rarely encounter the kind of traffic intensity found on University, Colorado Boulevard, or 6th Avenue. It's not that you couldn't safely ride those streets, but rather that you'll have more fun and feel safer on streets of lower traffic intensity. The more clearly you communicate your direction and needs, and the better you anticipate the intentions of the drivers around you, the safer and more enjoyable will be your time on the roads. Be a Buddha behind the bike. In the face of overwhelming power, use the cyclist's natural advantages—flexibility, maneuverability, and stopping power—to protect yourself. And by all means, get yourself out on the streets and ride there. I'm convinced that more cyclists on the roads mean greater safety for every cyclist. The more we become regular fixtures on the road, the better accustomed drivers become to our patterns of behavior and the more likely they will give us the space we need to feel safe around them.

Notes

1. Tom Vanderbilt, *Traffic: Why We Drive the Way We Do (And What It Says About Us)* (New York: Knopf, 2008).
2. Robert Hurst, *The Art of Cycling: A Guide to Bicycling in 21st-Century America*, 2nd. ed. (Guilford, CT: Falcon, 2006).
3. If you're interested, the Colorado traffic code can be found at §§ 42-4-101-2204.
4. "If the right-hand lane then available for traffic is wide enough to be safely shared with overtaking vehicles, a bicyclist shall ride *far enough to the right as judged safe by the bicyclist* to facilitate the movement of such overtaking vehicles unless other conditions make it unsafe to do so." Colo. Rev. Stat. § 42-4-1412(5)(a)(I) (emphasis added).
5. Colo. Rev. Stat. § 42-4-1412(5)(b)(I).
6. These changes are found scattered among Colo. Rev. Stat. §§ 42-4-1002-1005, -1008.5, and § 18-19-116.
7. And there's some research to back it up. See chapter 7 in *Listening to Bike Lanes* by Jeffrey A. Hiles. Available at www.wright.edu/~jeffrey.hiles/essays/listening/contents.html. "But when riding against the flow, road riders had twice the risk and sidewalk riders had four times the risk of those riding the same direction as the motor traffic on their side of the street."
8. Vanderbilt, *Traffic*, 178. "Roundabouts drop the number of potential conflicts to sixteen…and eliminate entirely the two most dangerous moves in an intersection—crossing through…and making a left turn."
9. Denver Rev. Mun. Code, § 54-576.
10. Hurst, *Art of Cycling*, 73.
11. Vanderbilt, *Traffic*, 199.
12. I am indebted to Bob Mionske, a lawyer, cyclist, and columnist, for the idea. http://bicyclelaw.com/road-rights/a.cfm/road-rights-a-stop-sign-solution, July 28, 2009.
13. Colo. Rev. Stat. § 42-4-612(1); Denver Rev. Mun. Code §54-107. The state statute says: "Whenever a driver approaches an intersection and faces a traffic control signal which is inoperative or which remains on steady red or steady yellow during several time cycles, the rules controlling entrance to a through street or highway from a stop street or highway, as provided under section 42-4-703, shall apply until a police officer assumes control of traffic or until normal operation is resumed. In the event that any traffic control signal at a place other than an intersection should cease to operate or should malfunction as set forth in this section, drivers may proceed through the inoperative or malfunctioning signal only with caution, as if the signal were one of flashing yellow."

Major Metro Trail Systems and Legend

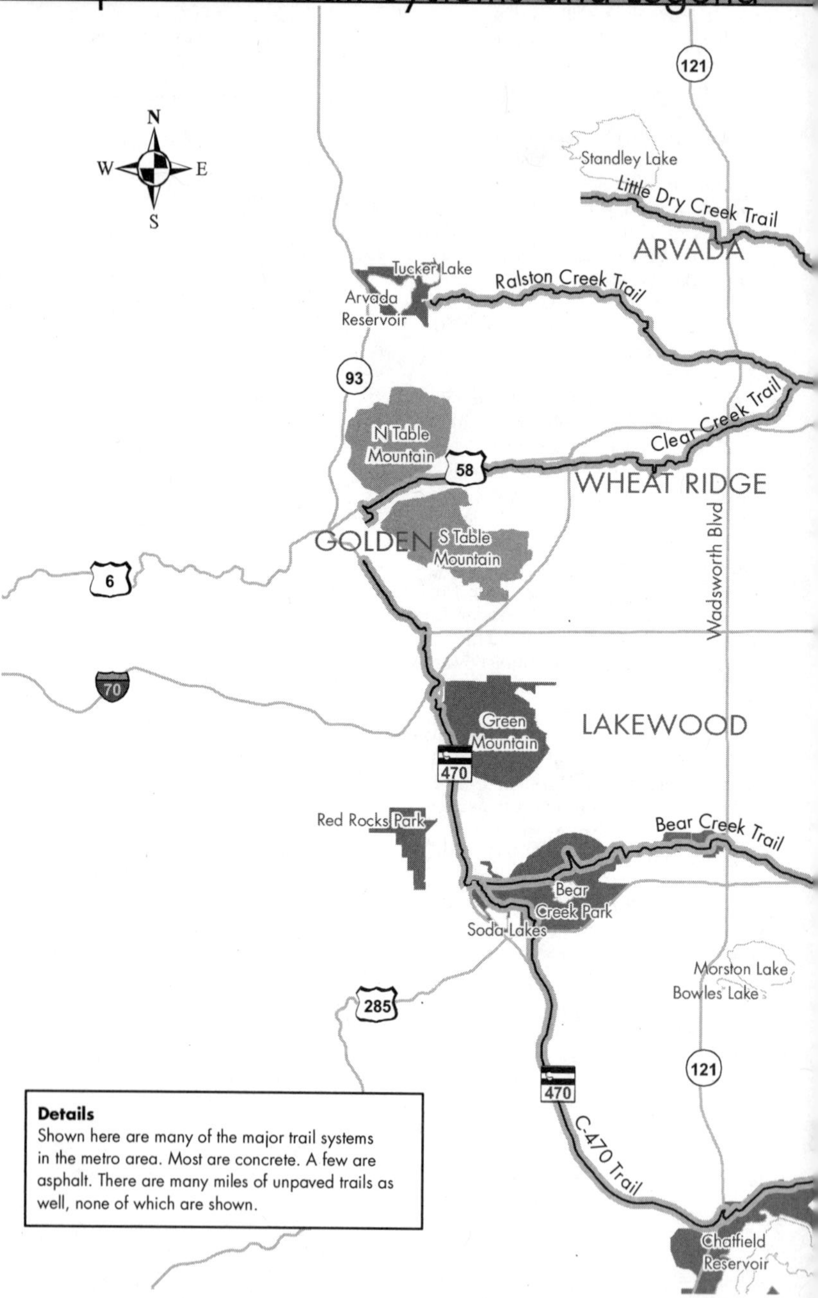

N
W · E
S

121

Standley Lake
Little Dry Creek Trail
ARVADA

Tucker Lake
Ralston Creek Trail
Arvada
Reservoir

93

Clear Creek Trail

N Table
Mountain

58

WHEAT RIDGE

GOLDEN   S Table
Mountain

6

Wadsworth Blvd

70

Green
Mountain

LAKEWOOD

470

Bear Creek Trail

Red Rocks Park

Bear
Creek Park

Soda Lakes

Morston Lake
Bowles Lake

285

121

470

C-470 Trail

Details
Shown here are many of the major trail systems
in the metro area. Most are concrete. A few are
asphalt. There are many miles of unpaved trails as
well, none of which are shown.

Chatfield
Reservoir

NORTHGLENN

Adams County
Open Space

COMMERCE CITY

Platte River Trail

Platte River Trail

Sand Creek Trail

DENVER

Cherry Creek Trail

Washington Park

Highline Canal Trail

AURORA

ENGLEWOOD

Cherry Creek
Reservoir

GREENWOOD VILLAGE

Legend

Major Trail Systems

Highways and Roads

Parks and Open Space

Lakes and Reservoirs

Centennial Trail

Major Metro Trail Systems and Legend 11

Equity Union Granary Terminal, Commerce City

Route Descriptions and Maps

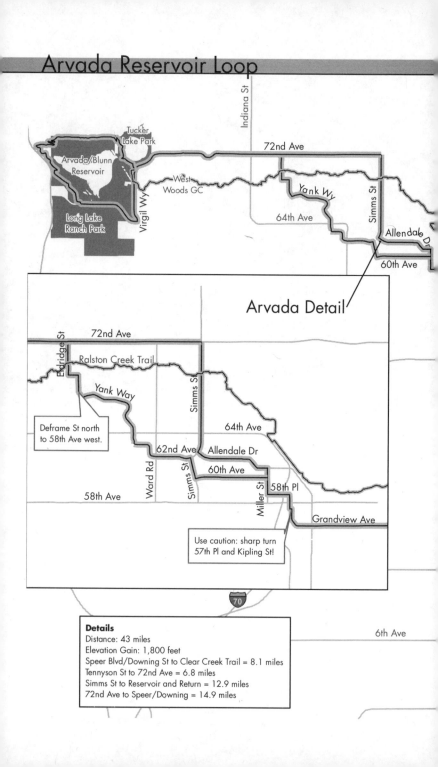

Arvada Reservoir Loop

Tucker Lake Park

Arvada/Blunn Reservoir

West Woods GC

Long Lake Ranch Park

Virgil Wy

72nd Ave

Indiana St

Yank Wy

64th Ave

Simms St

Allendale Dr

60th Ave

Arvada Detail

Eldridge St

72nd Ave

Ralston Creek Trail

Yank Way

Deframe St north to 58th Ave west.

Simms St

64th Ave

62nd Ave

Allendale Dr

Ward Rd

Simms St

60th Ave

Miller St

58th Pl

58th Ave

Grandview Ave

Use caution: sharp turn 57th Pl and Kipling St!

70

6th Ave

Details
Distance: 43 miles
Elevation Gain: 1,800 feet
Speer Blvd/Downing St to Clear Creek Trail = 8.1 miles
Tennyson St to 72nd Ave = 6.8 miles
Simms St to Reservoir and Return = 12.9 miles
72nd Ave to Speer/Downing = 14.9 miles

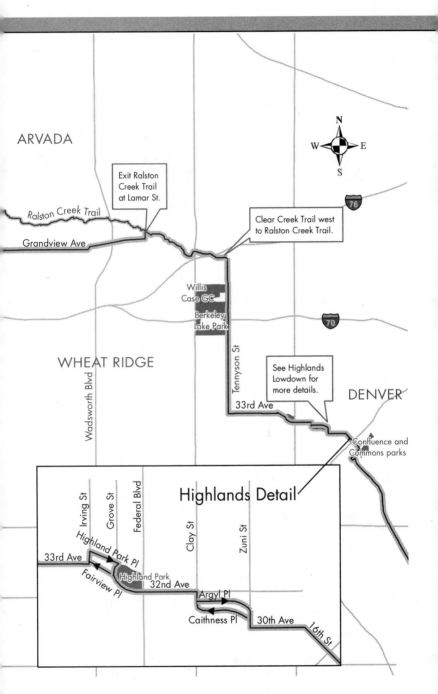

ARVADA

Exit Ralston Creek Trail at Lamar St.

Ralston Creek Trail

Grandview Ave

Clear Creek Trail west to Ralston Creek Trail.

Willis Case GC

Berkeley Lake Park

WHEAT RIDGE

Wadsworth Blvd

Tennyson St

See Highlands Lowdown for more details.

33rd Ave

DENVER

Confluence and Commons parks

Highlands Detail

Irving St

Grove St

Federal Blvd

Clay St

Zuni St

Highland Park Pl

33rd Ave

Fairview Pl

Highland Park

32nd Ave

Argyl Pl

Caithness Pl

30th Ave

16th St

Arvada Reservoir Loop

Distance: 43 miles
Elevation gain: 1,800 feet, most of it
   outbound to Arvada
Location: Northwest
Surface: 80% streets, but can be done as
   80% trails
Route finding: Advanced. The first time
   through North Denver and Arvada is likely
   to be slower than normal as you make your
   way through unfamiliar waypoints.
Traffic: Light to moderate most times of day.
   Use caution at W. 57th Pl. and Kipling St.—
   there is an extremely difficult hairpin turn on
   a narrow sidewalk.
Direction: Out-and-back route plus loop,
   with variations

Who knew that Arvada was such a great town for cycling? Arvada has long been known for featuring outstanding regional theater, dance, and music at the Arvada Center, and it's home to a couple of decent golf courses and a nicely preserved town center. But discovering both the quality and quantity of good road rides in this northwestern suburb is certainly one of the highlights of exploring the metro area for this guidebook. In recognition of its 189 miles of off-street trails and 74 miles of on-street routes, the League of American Bicyclists recently gave Arvada bronze certification as a bike-friendly town. More important to us, 50 percent of Arvada's arterial streets have bike lanes for cyclists, and the side streets have not been ruined by an overzealous application of stop signs.

This route begins near Washington Park, and then climbs up out of the Platte River drainage to take in the North Denver neighborhoods of Highland, West Highland, and Berkeley before it descends down into the Clear Creek flats. From there it climbs steadily northwest, roughly parallel to Ralston Creek, to just shy of 6,000 feet at Arvada Reservoir.

Begin anywhere on the Cherry Creek Trail. The mapped route measures from the corner of University Boulevard and 1st Avenue, but only the portion beginning from Confluence Park is shown. At Confluence Park make your way across the river and slightly north to 16th Street. The different ways of negotiating this stretch are shown on the Confusion at the Confluence map. At

16th, head west and take the Highland Bridge across I-25. Climb the small hill up 16th past Lola restaurant and the former Olinger Mortuary complex. Bear left on 30th Avenue, right on Zuni Street for 1 block, then left again onto Caithness Place. Route finding here the first time is awkward, but worth it. A supplemental map, Highlands Lowdown, will help orient you. Caithness takes you through the old Scottish Highlands neighborhood, a 19th-century developer's idea of what would sell best to newcomers from the East. Like its mate Argyle Place, Caithness is short, narrow, one-way, tree-lined, and interesting. You'll emerge with North High School to your left. Make your way up Clay Street for 1 block to 32nd Avenue. Go left. Cross Federal Boulevard at the light and bend around Highland Park to Fairview Place, another tree-lined gem, to connect back to the grid again on 33rd. Go west on this pleasant street to Tennyson Street, then north.

The stretch of Tennyson from 33rd north to 52nd Avenue is an interesting study in urban renewal and gentrification. There are hip new restaurants (Parisi, Brasserie Felix), cool old restaurants (Cafe Brazil, Sabor Latino), seemingly more independent espresso shops than anywhere outside Rome itself, fine old buildings from the early 20th century (including one that houses a ballroom dancing studio), and a small park between 41st and 42nd avenues in honor of César Chávez. Look for the interesting decorative art around the base wall of the park itself. Traffic through here can be tight, and cars come and go from the parking lane without much thought, so it's a good time to be on your toes and avoid the door zone. Berkeley Lake Park, once part of a sprawling alfalfa farm, begins at 46th Avenue and starts the short climb up alongside Willis Case Golf Course. Be sure to glance west here as you ascend to admire the views of the Front Range. At 52nd you leave Denver for unincorporated Adams County. A short jog right, then left announces the transition. Some caution here is warranted.

Keep cruising downhill to Clear Creek and the Clear Creek Trail. Look for the at-grade crossing about .4 mile beyond 52nd. Go west on the trail and cruise along the creek. Look for the start of the Ralston Creek Trail about .5 mile from Tennyson. The entrance to Arvada is marked by both a white suspension bridge and an enormous concrete-recycling plant. Stay on the Ralston Creek Trail for .9 mile until you come to a couple of big bridges over the trail; one is Lamar Street, the other Ralston Road. Make a decision here: stay on Ralston Creek for another 10 miles or get off here and ride to the reservoir on streets. Both routes are shown on the map. Only the street version is described, as it is faster, less serpentine, less crowded, and far more interesting. Route finding is slightly more difficult on the streets, but I've also managed to lose my way on Ralston Creek; confusingly, the trail is sometimes on both sides of the creek, there are a couple of at-grade street crossings that are not well marked, and as you near the reservoir you have to negotiate your way through two golf courses. If you do head out on Ralston Trail, rejoin the ride at Virgil Way, just before beginning the climb to the reservoir.

Exit Ralston Creek Trail at Lamar and go south .2 mile to Grandview Avenue. John Ralston, for whom the creek and trail are named, discovered a small amount of gold nearby in 1858 and helped touch off the huge influx of easterners in the late 19th century that forever transformed our state. Go right, heading west. Grandview ranks high on my personal list of the great stretches of road for cycling in the metro area. It's lined with trees and old houses, and there are wide shoulders, few interruptions, and a 30 mph speed limit. Stay on Grandview for a little more than 2 miles. You'll pass through Arvada's town center, where you'll likely encounter some traffic, but it's an imperceptible blip in this ride. At the cemetery the road bends right, becomes Johnson Street, and dead-ends at 57th Place. Go left 1 short block and find the bikes/pedestrians-only pass-through to Kipling. Use caution here as you make a sharp hairpin turn to the right on a very narrow sidewalk. Ride Kipling north across 58th Avenue through the edge of a shopping center (Starbucks is on your right), and exit left onto 58th Place. Cross Kipling Parkway.

At the T, go right on Miller Street for 4 blocks to Allendale Drive, another fine arterial with plenty of room for you and your bike. Turn left. Follow Allendale until it joins Simms Street, and go north to 72nd Avenue. This stretch may seem narrow and a little intimidating, but it's a designated bike route, so be as assertive as you need to be to protect yourself. Go left on 72nd. Stay on it all the way to Arvada Reservoir. This part of residential Arvada shades to rural. Horse trailers aren't uncommon, there are fields where hay is baled in old-fashioned rectangular bales, and you can smell a heady mix of grass, pollen, and cottonwoods.

Seventy-second morphs into Virgil Way as it bends south around Tucker Lake. Look for the trail on your right (there's a pedestrian crossing to indicate it) and start climbing. The climb isn't difficult; the views north, west, and south are extraordinary; and the path is in good shape.

After you've topped out, the trail winds down to the south side of the reservoir and a tunnel under 66th Avenue beckons. Ignore it, take the left fork, and climb back up to the avenue itself. Go left (east) toward Denver. Traffic on 66th is usually light but fast, and there's a good shoulder. At Virgil Way, climb back up to 72nd. Go east.

If you're not fed up with route finding, the map shows another interesting jaunt through Arvada for the return. Begin with a right on Eldridge Street, about .5 mile past Indiana Street. Go south on Eldridge, east at 68th Avenue, then south again on Deframe Street. Four blocks will bring you to Yank Street, a fine neighborhood stretch that winds south and east to 63rd Avenue (go left), south on Wright Street (past Faith Christian Academy), and east to 62nd Avenue. At Simms, go south to 60th Avenue, then east back to Miller and 58th Place, where you rejoin the outbound leg of the route. Return through the Highlands to Confluence Park by riding east on 33rd to Irving Street, then north to Highland Park Place, south around Highland Park to 32nd Avenue, and east on Argyle Place, all to accommodate the one-way streets in the area.

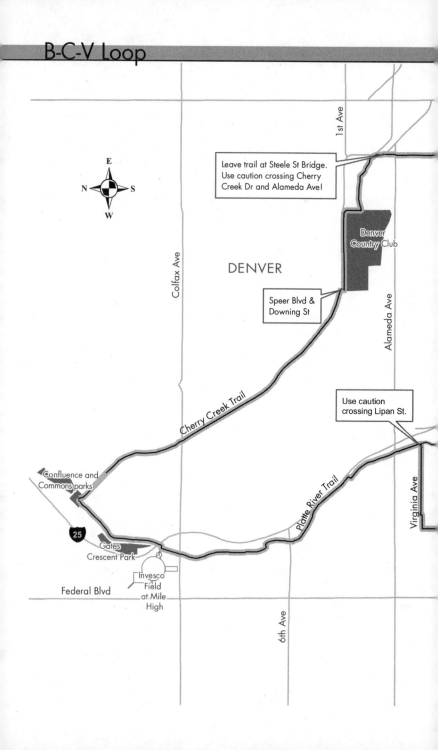

E
N — S
W

Leave trail at Steele St Bridge.
Use caution crossing Cherry
Creek Dr and Alameda Ave!

1st Ave

Denver
Country Club

Colfax Ave

DENVER

Speer Blvd &
Downing St

Alameda Ave

Cherry Creek Trail

Use caution
crossing Lipan St.

Confluence and
Commons parks

Platte River Trail

Virginia Ave

25

Gates
Crescent Park

Invesco
Field
at Mile
High

Federal Blvd

6th Ave

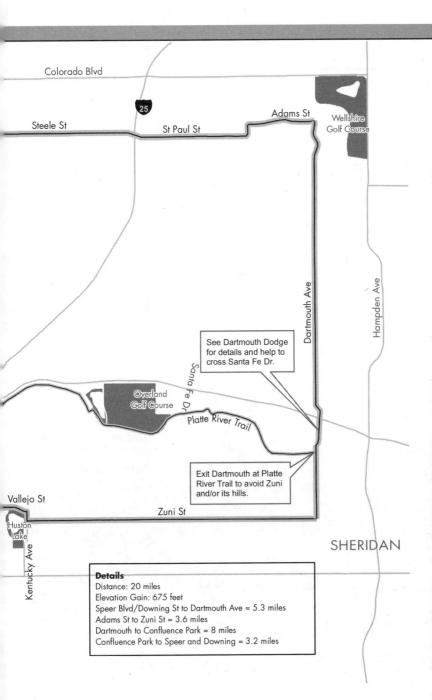

Colorado Blvd

25

Steele St   St Paul St   Adams St

Wellshire
Golf Course

Dartmouth Ave

Hampden Ave

See Dartmouth Dodge
for details and help to
cross Santa Fe Dr.

Santa Fe Dr

Overland
Golf Course

Platte River Trail

Exit Dartmouth at Platte
River Trail to avoid Zuni
and/or its hills.

Vallejo St

Zuni St

Huston
Lake

SHERIDAN

Kentucky Ave

Details
Distance: 20 miles
Elevation Gain: 675 feet
Speer Blvd/Downing St to Dartmouth Ave = 5.3 miles
Adams St to Zuni St = 3.6 miles
Dartmouth to Confluence Park = 8 miles
Confluence Park to Speer and Downing = 3.2 miles

B-C-V Loop

Distance: 20 miles

Elevation gain: 675 feet with the Zuni St. option

Location: Central

Surface: Up to 50% trails

Route finding: Easy

Traffic: Busiest on Dartmouth Ave. Ride it any time of day. Use caution when crossing Lipan St. at Virginia Ave.

Direction: Works well in both directions, save for a short stretch on Steele St. between Mississippi and Florida Aves. Clockwise is recommended.

B-C-V stands for *Belcaro, Cory-Merrill,* and *Valverde,* just three of the more than 15 neighborhoods this route takes you through. It works both as a gentle tour of the central and west-side neighborhoods, or can be extended by the addition of the loop along Zuni Street, one of the premier and underappreciated cycling streets in Denver. Short at 20 miles, B-C-V can be ridden after work or easily extended for a weekend workout. The hills along Zuni are a treat for those who like to climb.

Start at Speer Boulevard and Downing Street and head east along the Cherry Creek Trail to the Steele Street Bridge. Go right. Carefully cross Cherry Creek Drive, and work your way south across Alameda Avenue, a usually slow but busy street at rush hour. On your right, though difficult to see behind the walls and locked gates, are the homes, mostly built in the last 20 years, on the former polo grounds. When Denver expanded east and south from downtown at the end of the 19th century, recreation initially centered on the present-day Denver Country Club between University Boulevard and Downing. The golfers of the day, however, did not take kindly to those in their crowd who also wanted to play polo—the horses tended to tear up the turf. The polo crowd, by all accounts a gin-swilling bunch, decamped to the present location between Steele Street and University, Alameda, and Exposition avenues. If you want a better view of some of these homes, take a side trip from Exposition, Alameda, or University. Be forewarned, however, that unless you are stealthy, private security guards may impede your sightseeing progress.

Continue south on Steele and a small trail to and across Exposition into the heart of the Belcaro neighborhood. Named for the monstrous (33,000 square feet and 54 rooms) house at 3400 Belcaro Drive that Senator Lawrence Phipps built

A Zuni Street hill.

here in 1923, this neighborhood offers a great mix of interesting houses ranging from variations on the classic ranch to new interpretations of the international style. It's worth a short detour (east on Exposition, south on Belcaro) to ride by Phipps's retirement home. Continue south on Steele, crossing I-25, Buchtel Boulevard, and Evans Avenue. You're now on St. Paul Street, just east of the University of Denver in the University Park neighborhood, on your way to the Wellshire neighborhood. Just a few blocks to your west, across University, the houses are smaller. Many DU students live there. This side of the boulevard finds larger homes, many of which have been "popped," though not always with great success. If you have a moment, ride east on Wesley Avenue to Monroe Street and go a couple houses north to see one of the more interesting homes that's been constructed here. Otherwise, you'll come to the trickle of Harvard Gulch, where St. Paul stops. Jog left, then right again, and continue south on Adams Street to Dartmouth Avenue.

Go west on Dartmouth. It's good riding, has a designated bike lane most of the way, and even when you're in the industrialized area just west of the South Platte River, there's plenty of room for you and traffic. When you get to Santa Fe, use the Dartmouth Dodge to avoid delays and getting squeezed, then decide whether you want to return on the Platte River Trail or Zuni Street. I highly recommend Zuni as one of the most underrated cycling streets in Denver. It has several small rollers to keep you from getting bored, light traffic most of the time, and great views from the top of the climbs. Get out there and see something new! As you work your way north on Zuni, you'll come to Huston Lake Park at Kentucky Avenue, one of Denver's best, which will force you to detour east to Vallejo Street. Keep going north until Virginia Avenue, then go east, dropping fast back down to the Platte River. Use caution when crossing Lipan Street. Cross Jason Street to resume your journey on the Platte River Trail. The trail will return you to Confluence Park and then southeast back to where you started.

Bear Creek Park Loop

LAKEWOOD

Kipling Pkwy

Morrison Rd

Bear Creek Greenbe

Bear Creek Trail

MORRISON

Hampden Ave

Bear Creek
Lake Park

Belleview Ave

Wadsworth Blvd

Bowles Ave

Simms St

C-470 Trail

**Use caution! At-grade crossings
on Kipling Pkwy, Ken Caryl
Ave, Bowles, & Belleview Aves!**

Ken Caryl Ave

Chatfield Ave

Kipling Pkwy

Details
Distance: 44 miles
Elevation Gain: 1,800 feet
Speer Blvd/Downing St to Platte River Trail = 6.1 miles
Dartmouth Ave to C-470 Trail = 7.9 miles
Platte River Trail to Bear Creek Park Trail = 11.7 miles
Park Trail junction to Fox Hollow Golf Course = 3.3 miles
Fox Hollow GC to Platte River Trail = 8.5 miles

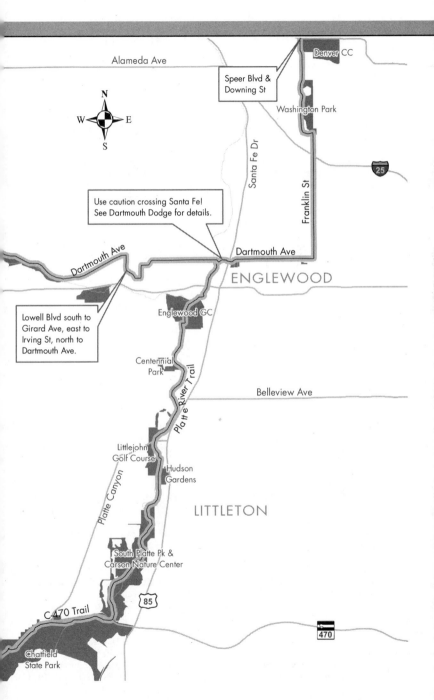

Alameda Ave

Denver CC

Speer Blvd &
Downing St

Washington Park

N
W   E
S

Santa Fe Dr

Franklin St

25

Use caution crossing Santa Fe!
See Dartmouth Dodge for details.

Dartmouth Ave

Dartmouth Ave

ENGLEWOOD

Englewood GC

Lowell Blvd south to
Girard Ave, east to
Irving St, north to
Dartmouth Ave.

Platte River Trail

Centennial
Park

Belleview Ave

Littlejohn
Golf Course

Platte Canyon

Hudson
Gardens

LITTLETON

South Platte Pk &
Carson Nature Center

85

C 470 Trail

470

Chatfield
State Park

Bear Creek Park Loop

Distance: 44 miles
Elevation gain: 1,800 feet
Location: Southwest
Surface: 75% trails
Route finding: Moderate
Traffic: Cycle traffic is heavy on the Platte and Bear Creek trails on the weekend.
Direction: Both

This long ride takes in the Platte River Trail and a major chunk of the C-470 Trail before returning to Denver on the Bear Creek Trail. It features great views of Chatfield Reservoir and the hogback ridge where the plains meet the mountains, then drops you into Lakewood's Bear Creek Park, a gem just east of Morrison. Were you so inclined, you could do almost the entire loop on trails (by following the Cherry Creek Trail to Confluence Park, then south on the Platte River Trail), but why would you? The short street sections south from Washington Park and along Dartmouth Avenue are mostly low traffic, and you shouldn't miss the climb up to and around Loretto Heights.

Begin by cruising down to and through Washington Park, exiting southeast at Franklin Street to pass by South High School. At Dartmouth go west and use the Dartmouth Dodge to access the Platte River Trail southbound. It's just short of 8 miles from Dartmouth to the C-470 Trail. The trail is smooth and even, and you'll pass through a number of golf courses and riverside parks before you hit Chatfield State Park and Reservoir. At Hampden Avenue you pass through a newly worked stretch of the trail, courtesy of the River Point Shopping Center just to the west. The trail slips along and through the Englewood Golf Course, its east side once the site of a major landfill from which methane used to periodically burble up, causing brown and lumpy fairways in the summertime. (Reconstruction in 2007 may have addressed the issue permanently.) Shortly before Union Avenue there is a series of small drops in the river, collectively known by kayakers as the Union Chutes. In the spring, if the water is up, you'll see multiple boaters getting an early-season fix. Use caution here, as the kayakers usually walk back up to the topmost drop while carrying their kayaks

on their shoulders and they probably will not see or hear you coming.

The most beautiful stretch of the South Platte Trail is along the last 2 to 3 miles. You're surrounded on both sides by native cottonwoods, and there's an abundance of small reservoirs and ponds with lots of fish, fowl, and fishermen. You'll occasionally see rafters, kayakers, and canoeists making their way down from C-470 to Bowles Avenue. The water here is relatively clean, the paddling is straightforward, and there are numerous small dams that were breached for safety in the 1970s. It's a fine way to while away a few hours on a hot summer day.

At C-470 you pass under the highway (tight quarters here) and bend west to join the C-470 Trail. A small climb takes you along the north side of Chatfield State Park, a Bureau of Reclamation project that finally got built after the huge flood of 1965. It serves many water-related purposes, including storage and flood control, but for most of the metro area it's a huge 5,000-acre recreation area with camping, hiking, cycling, boating, and dog walking all possible within the park proper. The views start to get impressive as you climb to the top of the dam, especially in the fall as the scrub oak in the foothills starts to turn. Descend from the high point about .5 mile and go right, through a tunnel under the highway. Immediately upon exiting, the trail turns back on itself to run west, parallel to the highway, and then alongside Wadsworth Boulevard, under which another tunnel provides safe passage. The serious climbing begins about here. From your low point at the junction of the Platte Trail and the C-470 Trail to the high point overlooking Bear Creek Park, your total gain is about 650 feet over a 12-mile stretch. It's not difficult, just slow. The views are fabulous: south is the blue expanse of Chatfield, west the foothills and the hogback ridge, where the plains end and the mountains begin, and east and north the plains, which stretch out past the housing developments and golf courses. Good views of downtown Denver are possible if the weather cooperates. Don't get too distracted, though. Much of the concrete in this stretch is in poor condition, with large settlement cracks badly filled with tar. Use caution, especially if you're passing or being passed.

The other distractions here are the four at-grade crossings you must make, at Kipling Parkway, Ken Caryl Avenue, Bowles Avenue, and Belleview Avenue. Drivers here are just getting on and off the highway, and their speeds are deceptively fast. At Marlowe Avenue the trail leaves the highway and runs alongside Eldridge Street, then disappears altogether for a couple of blocks.

Climbing tops out just past Quincy Avenue, and then the trail resumes and plunges down into the Bear Creek drainage and into the park itself. The Bear Creek Reservoir and Dam were created courtesy of the Army Corps of Engineers in 1980 as a way to seal the coffin on any possible floods into the metro area. To your left are Big and Little Soda lakes, to your right the reservoir. Work your way down the switchbacks. At the bottom decide whether to go west, around the lake, or east, directly to the dam face itself. The distance is slightly longer going west, but you'll see more of the park and the climbing is slightly easier. To the east, however, it's all trail, so you don't have to share the road with any cars. If you go east, about halfway up the dam's face the trail splits left and right. Go left! The right fork leads back south to Simms Street. As you top out, another trail junction appears. Go right and descend a steep and windy path. Both routes will wind you down and through portions of the Fox Hollow Golf Course before dumping you unceremoniously near the clubhouse on what used to be Old Morrison Road. Ride out to the end of the road and make a U-turn to join the Bear Creek Trail.

The Bear Creek Trail winds its way back and forth across the creek for about 2.75 miles before you pass under Wadsworth. This is a pleasant stretch shared by walkers, mountain bikers, and horses. It's hard to go very fast through here, however, so slow down and enjoy the trail's cool greenery. At Wadsworth you should, but don't need to, leave the trail and ride home from here on Dartmouth. If you cannot stand the streets, however, stay on the trail and just keep going until you reach the Platte River Trail. It's not much farther to go this way, but may be a little slower on account of the park you'll be riding through and the condition of the trail in a couple of places.

If you're up for some street riding and two more small hills, then by all means leave the trail and head east on Dartmouth after you pass under Wadsworth and after crossing the creek on a wooden bridge. This stretch (about 1.75 miles) seems made for cyclists: it's wide, the park borders one side, and there are few stop signs or other interruptions. At Sheridan Boulevard traffic intensity picks up briefly as you make your way east past a small shopping center that's seen better days. Keep riding east up Dartmouth to Lowell Boulevard. Go right, downhill around a sweeping S-turn. Go left on Girard Avenue for 1 block. Go left again on Irving Street and climb 2 blocks up to Colorado Heights University. Opened in 1891 as a Catholic boarding school, CHU sits on the highest piece of ground around (5,495 feet) and features a red sandstone tower that's more than 160 feet tall. Work your way east around the campus to the traffic light at Federal and Dartmouth. Use caution here. The light will not change for you unless there's a car with you. Head cautiously down Dartmouth. The hill is steep, the road surface is badly chopped up, there are rough railroad tracks at both Tejon and Shoshone streets, and there's something about a speeding bicycle that seems to engage drivers. Inexplicably, some will want to pass you, even if you're at or near the speed limit. When you arrive back at the Platte River, you're just a scant 4 miles from Washington Park. Remember to use the Dartmouth Dodge to avoid the Santa Fe intersection. A few small hills may challenge you before you turn left to Franklin, then it's a home stretch from there.

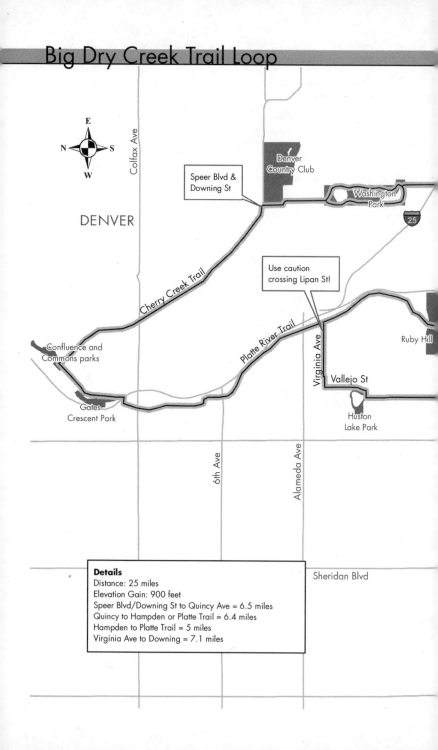

Big Dry Creek Trail Loop

Colfax Ave

N E S W

DENVER

Speer Blvd & Downing St

Denver Country Club

Washington Park

25

Cherry Creek Trail

Use caution crossing Lipan St!

Platte River Trail

Confluence and Commons parks

Gates Crescent Park

Virginia Ave

Vallejo St

Ruby Hill

Huston Lake Park

6th Ave

Alameda Ave

Sheridan Blvd

Details
Distance: 25 miles
Elevation Gain: 900 feet
Speer Blvd/Downing St to Quincy Ave = 6.5 miles
Quincy to Hampden or Platte Trail = 6.4 miles
Hampden to Platte Trail = 5 miles
Virginia Ave to Downing = 7.1 miles

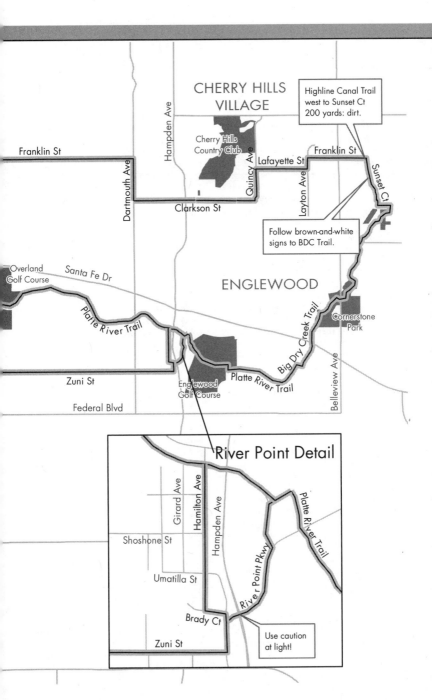

CHERRY HILLS VILLAGE

Hampden Ave

Cherry Hills Country Club

Quincy Ave

Franklin St

Dartmouth Ave

Lafayette St

Franklin St

Layton Ave

Sunset Ct

Clarkson St

Highline Canal Trail west to Sunset Ct 200 yards: dirt.

Follow brown-and-white signs to BDC Trail.

Overland Golf Course

Santa Fe Dr

ENGLEWOOD

Platte River Trail

Big Dry Creek Trail

Cornerstone Park

Zuni St

Englewood Golf Course

Platte River Trail

Belleview Ave

Federal Blvd

River Point Detail

Girard Ave

Hamilton Ave

Hampden Ave

Platte River Trail

Shoshone St

River Point Pkwy

Umatilla St

Brady Ct

Zuni St

Use caution at light!

Big Dry Creek Trail Loop

Distance: 25 miles
Elevation gain: 900 feet, most of it on Zuni St.
Location: South
Surface: 45% to 65% trails; balance on streets. Can be ridden 85% on trails if you forego the Zuni Hills.
Route finding: Moderate. Use caution when crossing Hampden Ave. at Brady Ct.
Traffic: Low to moderate nearly all the time
Direction: Both

This route invites you to consider F. Scott Fitzgerald's statement that the rich are different from you and me. From the extraordinary homes in Cherry Hills to the simple one-story brick houses along Zuni Street, you can ponder questions about class, race, and good views and bad—but most important, which neighborhood has better cycling potential. The route takes you directly south from Washington Park and then tours through a beautiful part of Cherry Hills Village, the part long-time residents refer to as Old Cherry Hills to distinguish it—and themselves, I suppose—from the nouveaux riches who populate Cherry Hills Village east of University Boulevard. To the untrained eye the differences are miniscule. Home to 6,000 well-educated and largely white people, the average household income in CHV is in excess of $200,000 and home values average $1.2 million. By contrast, the stretch along Zuni between Hampden and Alameda avenues has an average household income of around $40,000, is 60 percent to 75 percent Latino, and housing prices range between $75,000 and $250,000. After the CHV house tour, you'll ride along Big Dry Creek to reach the South Platte River Trail and work your way north and homeward. Highly recommended is the detour along Zuni. It has great hills, few stop signs or red lights, and provides stunning views east and west from the high grounds above the South Platte. The final legs of the loop bring you to Confluence Park and back up the Cherry Creek Trail.

Begin near Speer Boulevard and Downing Street. Head south immediately, first on Downing, then on Marion Parkway, through Washington Park, and out on Franklin Street past South High School toward the University of Denver. Go west on Dartmouth and south again on Clarkson Street. This can be slightly busy due to traffic in and around Swedish and Craig hospitals. (The latter, which cares for and rehabilitates patients with spinal cord and traumatic brain injuries, is routinely ranked as one of the top 10 hospitals in the world.) Cross Hampden, go south about 1 mile, and turn left on Quincy Avenue. Ignore the path/trail on the north side of the street. You'll only be on Quincy for .3 mile before going south again on Lafayette Street. This and the stretch along Franklin are the heart of Cherry Hills Village. The houses are large, but not ostentatiously so, the grounds manicured, and there is usually enough land to permit the full panoply of suburban delights: swimming pools, tennis courts, soccer and lacrosse goals, and graceful curved driveways. This is a great place to fantasize about what you would do if you won the lottery and how you'd landscape your own acre of land. The streets here are narrow lanes, but traffic volume is low and drivers benign. Go left on Layton Avenue and right on Franklin.

Franklin intersects with the Highline Canal Trail after .7 mile, shortly after crossing Belleview Avenue. It's an easy turn to miss, and marked only by a wooden bridge, a crosswalk, and a sign poorly placed to read from Franklin. Turn right onto the well-traveled and hard-packed trail. If you miss the turn you'll know soon, for Franklin shortly dead-ends at Crestridge Drive. Ride along the canal and soak up the ambience. Go about .5 mile and look for a narrow dirt path to the right. Take it. It leads you out west to Sunset Court, Sunset Lane, and south on Washington Street. Follow the obvious brown-and-white signs to the Big Dry Creek Trail, south on Washington to Powers Avenue and right. Join the trail. Stay on it until you come to the South Platte River. The BDC Trail is in great shape and winds through a number of south suburban parks, open spaces, and playing fields, one of which features a pint-size train into which small kids are crammed for a short loop around the park. Pity the poor Lion's Club volunteer in 90° weather dressed in his obligatory striped pants.

The BDC Trail joins the South Platte Trail just after the dog park. Go right. Head north through the Union Chutes area (where kayakers can be found in the spring) and navigate through the Englewood Golf Course. At its north side, cross the river and decide whether to continue north on the Platte River Trail or to detour out to the Zuni Hills. If you choose the former, continue north to Confluence Park, about 8 miles, then return to Speer and Downing via the Cherry Creek Trail. This stretch is more fully described in the Platte River Trail South route description.

For Zuni Street, leave the Platte Trail after crossing the river and go left on the access street in front of you, River Point Parkway. Follow it out past the movie theater, negotiate the roundabouts, and bear right. Stop at Hampden and reconnoiter. You need to cross US 285 here, go left for a short block on old Hampden Avenue, then right to reach Zuni. If you have a northbound car in your lane, great. The light will eventually cycle and give you a short green to cross. Watch for cars turning in front of you. Without a northbound car, however, you'll only get a left turn signal and southbounders will have a left turn signal, leaving you caught betwixt and between. A pedestrian button on the western side of Brady will allow a safe crossing if all else fails. If this sounds unpleasant (it's really not that bad), ride north on the Platte River Trail under US 285 and go left on Hamilton Avenue. Ride it west and south 3 blocks to join old Hampden.

Go north on Zuni, one of the great cycling streets in Denver. A few lights and stop signs will slow your progress, but the many hills keep the interest high. Climbing from Hampden, you hit a high mark at Bates Avenue, from which there are great views east and west. Zuni rides well almost any time of day, but it's busiest during the early mornings as the many contractors and landscape crews based here head out to work. Keep riding north through the College View and Ruby Hill neighborhoods. At Kentucky Avenue go right, then left on Vallejo Street to circle Huston Lake Park. Continue north to Virginia Avenue. Go right and drop steeply down to rejoin the Platte River Trail. Cross Lipan and Jason streets with care for the railroad tracks and the traffic. Continue north on the trail to Confluence Park and the Cherry Creek Trail, 7 miles altogether back to Speer and Downing.

In case of rain, fatigue, or time constraints, you can shorten the loop by crossing the Platte at Mississippi Avenue (see the Mississippi Muddle), on the sidewalk of the 8th Avenue viaduct (watch for glass on the sidewalk), or at 13th Avenue. And if you've grown to dislike trails of all kinds, make your way north from Zuni on Tejon Street, 2nd Avenue, Yuma Street, 5th Avenue, Bryant Street, Canosa Court, and Decatur Street. This is a very busy truck area during the week, but it's deserted on the weekends and thus perfect for urban exploring.

Central Parks Trifecta

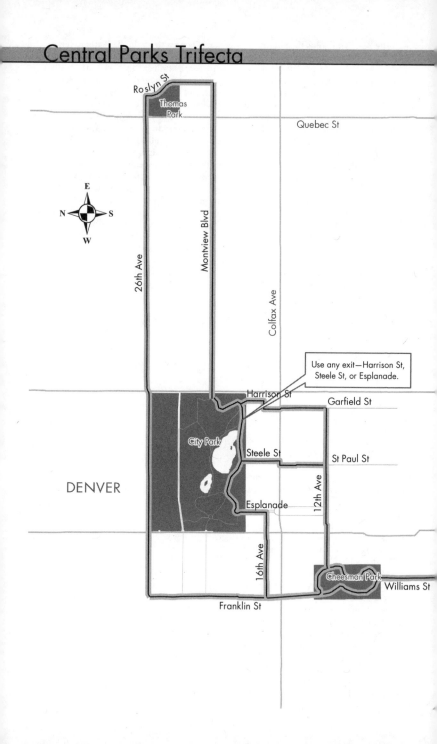

Roslyn St

Thomas Park

Quebec St

E
N — S
W

26th Ave

Montview Blvd

Colfax Ave

Use any exit—Harrison St, Steele St, or Esplanade.

Harrison St

Garfield St

City Park

Steele St

St Paul St

DENVER

12th Ave

Esplanade

16th Ave

Cheesman Park

Williams St

Franklin St

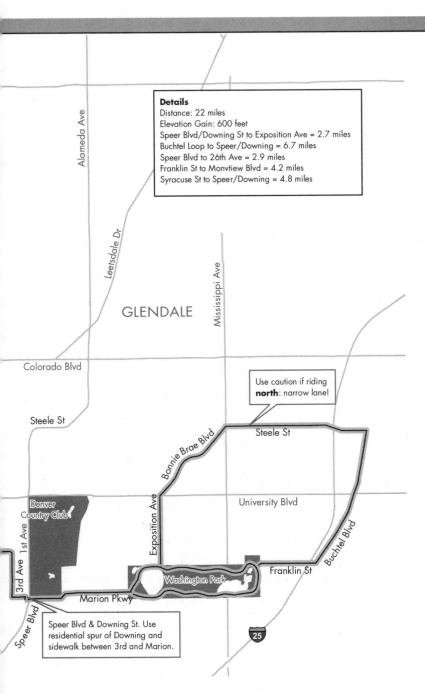

Details
Distance: 22 miles
Elevation Gain: 600 feet
Speer Blvd/Downing St to Exposition Ave = 2.7 miles
Buchtel Loop to Speer/Downing = 6.7 miles
Speer Blvd to 26th Ave = 2.9 miles
Franklin St to Monvtiew Blvd = 4.2 miles
Syracuse St to Speer/Downing = 4.8 miles

Alameda Ave

Leetsdale Dr

GLENDALE

Mississippi Ave

Colorado Blvd

Use caution if riding **north**: narrow lane!

Steele St

Steele St

Bonnie Brae Blvd

University Blvd

Denver
Country Club

1st Ave

Exposition Ave

Buchtel Blvd

3rd Ave

Washington Park

Franklin St

Marion Pkwy

Speer Blvd

Speer Blvd & Downing St. Use
residential spur of Downing and
sidewalk between 3rd and Marion.

25

Central Parks Trifecta

Distance: 22 miles (though many variations are possible)
Elevation gain: 600 feet
Location: Central
Surface: 75% streets; balance within the parks
Route finding: Easy
Traffic: Narrow and slow between Cheesman Park and 26th Ave. on Franklin St. Also narrow heading northbound on Steele St.
Direction: Both, but avoid northbound Steele St.

This route takes in three of the major parks in central Denver: Washington, City, and Cheesman. The on-street sections traverse multiple neighborhoods, cross several major thoroughfares, and give the less-experienced rider the feel of navigating his way to and from auto-free zones. You can start anywhere on the loop, add distance by adding additional loops, cut out a loop if you're feeling tired or want to avoid traffic on a particular section, and generally use the basic model to begin your own exploration of the streets and parks of Denver. With multiple loop options within and outside of each park, the variations are plentiful. The landscapes are gorgeous in all seasons. Auto traffic is not a huge issue, though park traffic can be congested, especially on the weekends and after work. Start anywhere. The description below starts in or near Washington Park.

Washington Park began life as open pastureland. An early ditch brought water to the area from southern Jefferson County. Different parcels were assembled between 1877 and 1905. The three major design elements are Smith and Grasmere lakes to the north and south and the Great Field in the middle, all joined together by a sinuous set of roadways that interweave throughout.

Beyond its obvious importance as a major anchor in the Denver park system, Washington Park is also the unofficial epicenter of road riding in the city (at least in terms of the sheer number of cyclists), a fact that has always been a puzzle to me. Home to huge contingents of soccer and volleyball players, runners, dog walkers, roller-bladers, children at play, Canada geese, and cyclists, Wash Park is not a great place to go fast. The nominal speed limit is 15 mph, and from time to time the park police will borrow a radar gun and crack down on speeding cyclists. In an effort to enforce some kind of order, Parks and Recreation has split the main loop road down the middle: the outer half is the province of all things wheeled and the inner half is reserved for pedestrians. Skateboarders and inline skaters occupy an uneasy zone of transition between foot-based and wheel-based recreation. Wheeled things go counterclockwise, pedestrians clockwise. One of my riding partners maintains a "dartsicle" watch whenever we ride through the park: kids (and adults) on bicycles who suddenly dart out in front of you. Also keep your eye out for tennis players crossing at the south end, and the women with baby joggers who organize for group exercise at established stations scattered around the park. It's a scene. Cars are allowed into the park at various points (north, west, and east), but use caution around them—they may be from out of town and completely starstruck by the inordinate number of beautiful men and women working their way around the park.

Start at Speer Boulevard and Downing Street. If you've come from the north, be sure to use the residential spur of Downing between 3rd Avenue and Speer, and then use the wide sidewalk on the eastern side of Downing to reach Marion Parkway. Use caution on Marion at Virginia, as the westbound drivers frequently have the sun in their eyes and most cars don't slow at the pedestrian crossing. Alameda to the north isn't much better. Circle the park and exit on the east side at Exposition Avenue. Go east to University Boulevard and angle diagonally right at the light to pick up Bonnie Brae Boulevard. There's fine sight-seeing through here, with an interesting mix of architectural styles that range from small bungalows to contemporaries. At the next light (Mississippi Avenue) head straight south on Steele Street. You'll soon pass a welcome bit of open space on your left, all of which is owned by the Catholic archdiocese. As you cross I-25, Steele bends west and morphs into St. Paul Street.

At Buchtel Boulevard turn right, either onto the eponymous historic bike path or the road proper, and ride a short distance to University. Cross with caution here, and ride northwest to Franklin Street to cross the interstate. To your left is the north edge of the University of Denver, its standards and reputation as a skiing and party school much improved from the last century. The RTD light-rail stops here, so it's a busy stretch. North on Franklin takes you alongside South High School, a fine example of Romanesque architecture and one of the four compass-point high schools built in the 1930s. Reenter the park at Franklin and head north to exit at Marion Parkway.

As you follow Marion and Downing north from Washington Park, you can begin to appreciate the early city planners' vision of a city connected through its parks by broad green parkways. Most of the parks and parkways were registered on the National Register of Historical Properties in 1986. Follow Marion north to where it curves into Downing. Keep going. Cross Speer and again use the residential spur of Downing to reach and go right on 3rd Avenue. A left on Gilpin Street takes you out of the Country Club neighborhood through a set of fabulous arches to 4th Avenue. A quick right and left will take you to Williams Street and north to the Cheesman Esplanade, the entrance to Cheesman Park.

Cheesman Park began life as a dusty high spot well outside the city boundary. The early settlers staked out the Mt. Prospect Cemetery in 1858. Thirty years later the city had expanded, a rival and better-irrigated cemetery had been developed along the Platte at Riverside Cemetery, and the graveyard had become (or remained) run-down, dusty, and underappreciated. To convert the land from a cemetery for Protestants (Catholics and Jews were buried to the east) to a park took an act of Congress, but eventually an undertaker was hired to disinter the 5,000 bodies in the park and move them to Riverside Cemetery. The undertaker found the undertaking not to his liking: the work was too hard and the pay too little. A scandal erupted when it was discovered that he'd been cramming three or four sets of remains into a single small coffin to speed up the process and cut down on expense. An estimated 2,000 to 3,000 remains still remain there.

Cheesman Park has great views of the mountains and no organized athletic events due to its sloping central fields. The loop through the park is narrow, but the auto traffic is generally benign. Roll north out of the park on Franklin, then cross Colfax (the longest street in the United States by someone's reckoning) and work your way on narrow streets through the hospital district. This is a slow stretch, with many stop signs, lights, and traffic. Use caution.

Once you've gotten to 26th Avenue, you're home free. Head east, and you'll soon have an uninterrupted stretch from York Street to Colorado Boulevard along the north side of City Park Golf Course on which to work your legs. Cross Colorado. Keep going. North and south is Greater Park Hill. Twenty-sixth used to be the color line in Denver, in the last century dividing white and black citizens after African Americans spilled out of Five Points and moved east. Cross Quebec Street, go east to Roslyn Street, turn right, and head 6 blocks south (Roslyn becomes Syracuse) to Montview Boulevard. Go west on Montview for 2 miles, cross Colorado, and enter City Park.

City Park is a wondrous place. Perhaps the greatest wonder is why so few cyclists use it. It has great variety, interesting loop combinations, and less traffic than Washington Park. Three roundabouts with fine concrete surfaces will speed your progress, though a few metal barriers with narrow openings will impede it. Watch for the Civil War–era replicas of mortars and cannons. Near the tennis courts there's often a game of handball being played, but handball with a distinctly Latino flair. The men wear thin wooden paddles on each hand and beat the heck out of a bouncy rubber ball. Three exits leave the park to the south: at the Esplanade, Steele Street, and Harrison Street. Take either of the first two to 12th Avenue, then go west through a quiet commercial strip in the Congress Park neighborhood and west to Cheesman Park. Or reverse your tracks to Franklin Street along 16th Avenue and Franklin. From Cheesman it's an easy jaunt down Williams to Speer and Downing again.

Cherry Creek Anti-Trail Loop

Speer Blvd &
Downing St

Denver
Country Club

Alameda Ave

GLENDALE

Washington
Park

DENVER

Monaco Blvd

Colorado Blvd

Franklin St

University Blvd

Use east sidewalk between
Hampden & Dartmouth.

Dartmouth Ave

Dahlia St

ENGLEWOOD

Wellshire GC

Hampden Ave

Happy Canyon Rd

Use caution
at light!

Colorado Blvd

CHERRY HILLS VILLAGE

Quincy Ave

Monaco St

Kent Denver School

Use caution
at light!

Details
Distance: 32 miles
Elevation Gain: 1,200 feet
Speer Blvd/Downing St to Colo Blvd = 6 miles
Colo Blvd to Monaco St = 2.5 miles
Monaco to Reservoir = 2.6 miles
Reservoir Loop = 9 miles

Belleview Ave

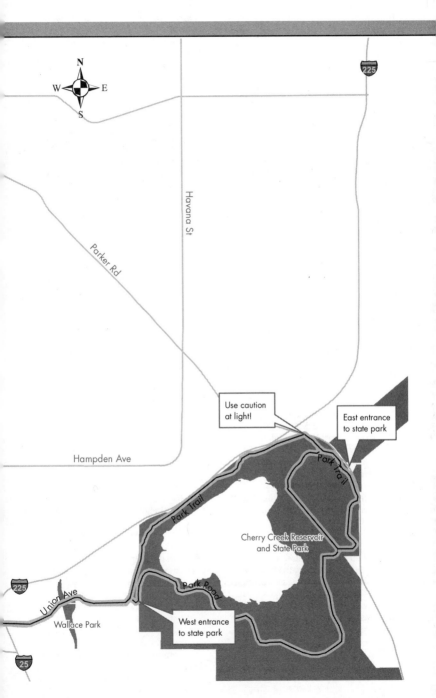

Cherry Creek Anti-Trail Loop

Distance: 32 miles

Elevation gain: 1,200 feet, spread out through the middle of the ride in the form of gentle rollers

Location: Southeast

Surface: 90% streets; balance on park roads and trails

Route finding: Moderate. Use caution while crossing Hampden Ave. at Colorado Blvd. and at Cherry Creek Dam Rd.

Traffic: Although designed to take advantage of low weekend traffic, this route can be ridden any time of day.

Direction: The ride is a double lollipop, with two loops to consider. Go in both directions to keep things interesting.

It's no secret to my riding friends that I'm not wild about bike trails. Sure, I use them when I have to, or when I don't want to ride in traffic, but for the most part I like riding on the streets. There's more to notice and it's a better experience, whether because of the scenery, architecture, people, or interaction with other riders and cars. While the Cherry Creek Trail is a thing of wonder, I avoid it when I can, especially so because the below-grade portions of the trail feel claustrophobic and on weekends it's neither courteous nor safe to ride very fast. There are too many kids, families, and dogs.

This route came from a wish to visit the Cherry Creek Reservoir without riding the Cherry Creek Trail. It starts in Washington Park, heads south on Franklin Street through the University of Denver neighborhood, turns east at Dartmouth Avenue, and works its way out to the reservoir through the Denver Tech Center.

When Denver was growing and becoming car-centric and suburban, new development moved south and east. When thousands fled Denver in the face of forced busing in the 1970s, many moved to Arapahoe County to live within the Cherry Creek School District. Although genteel and self-congratulatory, the neighborhoods make for great riding, flat at the beginning and end but punctuated with moderate rollers that can keep your heart rate up.

Begin near Washington Park. Head south out of the park on Franklin, past South High School. Franklin takes you south through DU to Dartmouth. Turn east toward Colorado Boulevard and work your way up the first of many rollers. Cross Colorado, either with the light and the crosswalk or get up your courage to make a right and then an *immediate* left from the middle lane to rejoin the continuation of Dartmouth on the east side of Colorado. Be brave here: it's not as hard as it looks. Because of the turn lane on Colorado, you're only crossing three lanes at a time and can pause as long as you need to check the closing speed of drivers coming north. Follow Dartmouth slightly north and east to Dahlia Street. Turn right and climb another small hill to Hampden Avenue. Cross Hampden diagonally with the light and traffic to Happy Canyon Road. Happy Canyon has a dedicated bike lane and climbs gradually to a traffic light at Monaco Street. Along the way you can admire Thomas Jefferson High School and yet another of Denver Water's underground storage facilities—no water visible, just open space. It's at the top of the hill, naturally.

Go right at Monaco. It's three, then two lanes wide and traffic is light on the weekends. At Union Avenue, go left. It'll take you all the way out to the reservoir. From a watershed perspective, you've just climbed out of the Platte and Cherry Creek drainages and are dropping into the Goldsmith Gulch drainage as you crest Happy Canyon. But not for long. As you pass through the heart of the Tech Center you bottom out and pass a gorgeous park (Wallace Park, named for the founder of the Denver Tech Center) as you climb out to the Cherry Creek drainage again. Cross Yosemite, pass Cherry Creek High School, and go right on Dayton Street to enter the state park at the western entrance. Ride downhill on the park road and bear right to circumnavigate the park. The road is only in fair shape, with many frost heaves to disrupt your ride. But it's all you have, so go east, then climb north on it to the T-intersection. Go right, and keep climbing to the next intersection. Go straight across. The road bends west and downhill. (You can also go right at this intersection, ride out to the west entrance of the park, then cut left along the park trail.) Just short of 1 mile, look for a concrete trail to your right. Take it. For all my grousing about trails, the one here is a good one: concrete, wide, and well maintained. It rolls through a beautiful, relatively unspoiled stretch of the park, replete with native shrubs and towering cottonwood trees. The trail leaves the park at Cherry Creek Dam Road. The crossing is decidedly unfriendly. Aggressive drivers approach from three directions, and two directions usually have green lights (by design; it's a T-intersection). Use caution. If traffic is heavy, use the button and cross on the walk signal.

Descend to the intersection with the Cherry Creek Trail, slowing down for the sharp left turn to ride along the face of the dam. There's frequently a fine layer of sand that has been washed down here, so use caution as you make the turn. Follow the perimeter of the park on the trail until you return to the west entrance of the park, another gradual climb. Retrace your steps to the Monaco–Happy Canyon intersection. Immediately after turning left on Happy Canyon, *stay on the left side of the single lane* (drivers may not like it, but do it anyway) and make a hard left to Quincy Avenue. Settle in to the Little Dry Creek drainage. Stay on Quincy all the way to Colorado and enjoy the spin through Cherry Hills Village. There's a bike path to the south, but why would you? The road is all downhill, the speed limit is only 30 mph, and with a little effort you can come close to that and not feel guilty about holding up traffic. Besides, they can pass you. What a novel concept!

Turn right on Colorado and climb up and down to Hampden. Pause at the light. Pay attention. There's a lot going on here. Eastbound Hampden has a green light and arrow even as westbound Hampden has a red light. Cars behind you may want to turn right on red while you wait. Southbound Colorado has a double turn lane to accommodate those going east on Hampden, and they start while you lowly northbounders must wait. Cross *only* when you've got a green light. Look for a path/sidewalk on the right side of Colorado. This is your destination, but to get there you have to negotiate with drivers turning north on Colorado. They're a surly lot sometimes, so use caution. The path/sidewalk will carry you north up the last small hill to Dartmouth, and you're nearly home free.

Confirming my prejudice that one of the most dangerous place a cyclist can be is on the sidewalk, you have to negotiate a number of intersections along Colorado (all signed appropriately with stop signs) where drivers rarely will notice you. With obstructed views, full stops are suggested. Were these difficulties not enough of an insult to law-abiding cyclists, getting back to westbound Dartmouth is tricky, requiring you to choose between a hard-right/hard-left scenario or an awkward pedestrian crossing option. I'll confess here that on most weekends I usually cross Hampden at the light and forget about the sidewalk. I just keep going, sprinting up and down to the Dartmouth intersection where, if the traffic gods are smiling on me, I'll make a cool turn to Dartmouth with enough speed to carry me all the way back to flatland. On most slow weekends this is a good alternative—and if you get looks or worse from some of the drivers, just remind yourself, *There are three freaking lanes here!* Finish the ride by cruising back up Franklin to Washington Park, then onward to Speer and Downing.

Cherry Creek–Heather Gardens Loop

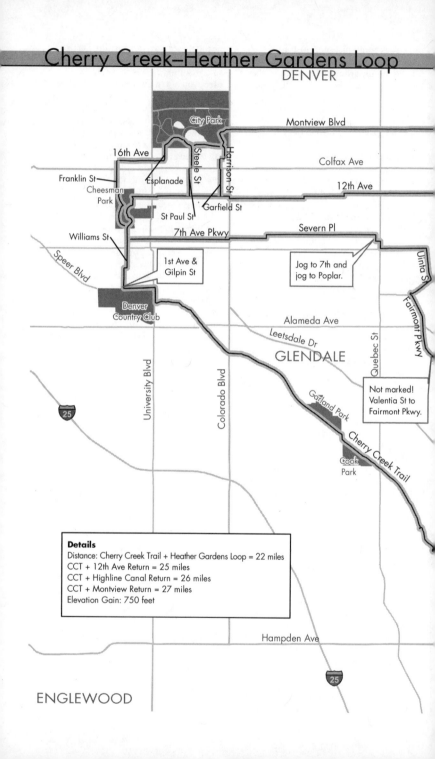

DENVER

City Park

Montview Blvd

16th Ave

Steele St

Harrison St

Colfax Ave

Franklin St

Esplanade

12th Ave

Cheesman Park

Garfield St

St Paul St

7th Ave Pkwy

Severn Pl

Williams St

Speer Blvd

1st Ave & Gilpin St

Jog to 7th and jog to Poplar.

Uinta St

Fairmont Pkwy

Denver Country Club

Alameda Ave

Leetsdale Dr

University Blvd

Colorado Blvd

GLENDALE

Quebec St

Not marked!
Valentia St to
Fairmont Pkwy.

25

Garland Park

Cherry Creek Trail

Cook Park

Details
Distance: Cherry Creek Trail + Heather Gardens Loop = 22 miles
CCT + 12th Ave Return = 25 miles
CCT + Highline Canal Return = 26 miles
CCT + Montview Return = 27 miles
Elevation Gain: 750 feet

Hampden Ave

25

ENGLEWOOD

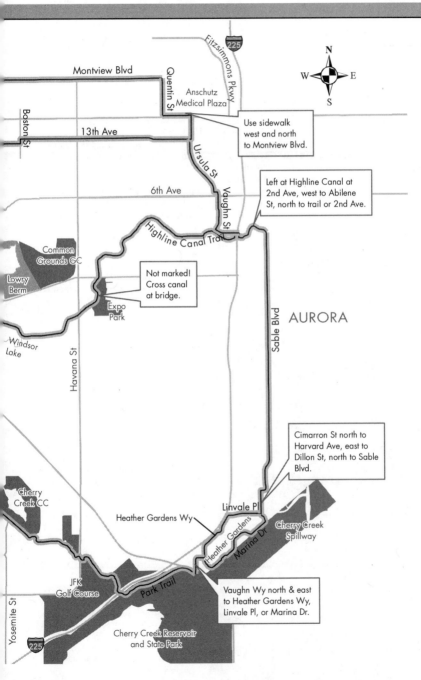

Montview Blvd

Quentin St

Anschutz
Medical Plaza

Use sidewalk
west and north
to Montview Blvd.

Boston St

13th Ave

Ursula St

6th Ave

Vaughn St

Left at Highline Canal at
2nd Ave, west to Abilene
St, north to trail or 2nd Ave.

Highline Canal Trail

Common
Grounds GC

Lowry
Berm

Not marked!
Cross canal
at bridge.

Expo
Park

Sable Blvd

AURORA

Windsor
Lake

Havana St

Cimarron St north to
Harvard Ave, east to
Dillon St, north to Sable
Blvd.

Cherry
Creek CC

Linvale Pl

Heather Gardens Wy

Heather Gardens

Marina Dr

Cherry Creek
Spillway

JFK
Golf Course

Park Trail

Vaughn Wy north & east
to Heather Gardens Wy,
Linvale Pl, or Marina Dr.

Yosemite St

Cherry Creek Reservoir
and State Park

Fitzsimmons Pkwy

225

Cherry Creek–Heather Gardens Loop

Distance: 22 to 27 miles
Elevation gain: 750 feet for the longest loop
Location: Southeast
Surface: Mix of streets and trails, depending on route selection
Route finding: Moderate. Use caution when crossing Cherry Creek Dam Rd.
Traffic: Light on weekends; moderate during the week
Direction: Both, but counterclockwise is slightly better when riding on Sable Blvd.

Once you've conquered the Cherry Creek Reservoir Loop, it's immediately time to start thinking of ways to avoid a return trip on the trail. Not that I'm anti-trail or anything, it's just that there's a huge world out there you're missing if you

spend your entire cycling life on the paths and trails. "There are more things in heaven and earth, Horatio, than are dreamt of in your philosophy." The following variation is a ride in itself, if you want it to be, into Aurora. On a slow Sunday the full loop along Sable and then Montview boulevards makes a fabulous circuit.

Tucked between I-225 and the Cherry Creek Reservoir spillway, Heather Gardens is a quiet retirement community, a fact you'll quickly deduce from the absence of swings, children, and footballs, the ultrawide streets, and the 25 mph speed limits. The area was developed in the 1970s, and it has that soulless feel common to the era: unimaginative architecture, repetitive forms, and in the office buildings nearby, glass and steel in rectilinear layouts. The Heather Gardens Loop around the golf course (which you really cannot see from the road) comes in at just under 3 miles plus 100 feet gained, but if you're adventurous, don't stop there. Central Aurora beckons, and on a slow traffic day (Sunday mornings, for instance) the ride up Sable Boulevard is well worth doing. It takes in a number of parks, passes near the central government structures, and eventually joins up with the Highline Canal Trail. From there you can return via the Canal Trail (slow; many at-grade crossings), 12th Avenue (a pleasant ride with many stops signs), or Montview Boulevard (a great option).

Ride to the reservoir. Go east when you reach the park trail. On the northeast curve of the Cherry Creek Reservoir there's an awkward intersection where Cherry Creek Dam Road intersects with South Vaughn Way. Start your adventure here. Cross the dam road and go north on Vaughn under Parker Road. Go right with Vaughn and right again onto Heather Gardens Way, which turns into East Marina Drive. Marina Drive winds around the golf course with views out into the bare spillway. On the north side it becomes Linvale Place and coming south again Heather Gardens Way. A final right at South Vaughn completes the loop and brings you back to the dam road.

Looking west across Cherry Creek Reservoir.

If you're ready to explore Aurora further, leave Marina Drive where it turns into Linvale and cross Yale Avenue on Cimarron Street, which dead-ends at Harvard Avenue. Turn right, and follow Harvard east and north. Harvard becomes Dillon Street, and at Iliff Avenue becomes Sable Boulevard. Ride north on Sable. From Iliff to Evans Avenue the riding is pleasant: there is one lane in either direction and pretty low traffic volume and intensity. At Jewell Avenue things pick up, with two lanes both north and south, a 35 mph speed limit, and no bike lane. Don't be shy here about taking as much of the right lane as you need to be safe. Tight conditions persist until Mississippi Avenue where a narrow but serviceable bike lane opens up. You can make good speed here. As you cross Alameda Avenue, look east for views of Aurora's City Hall and center of government. Watch for Ellsworth Avenue on your left, after which get ready to move to the left lane to cross to the Highline Canal Trail at approximately 2nd Avenue. This is a distinctly unfriendly crossing that moves diagonally across a raised median. Follow the trail to Abilene Street, go right on Abilene, and left almost immediately on 2nd to cross under I-225. The trail picks up again on your left after I-225, or just stay on 2nd until you're past Salem Street and can see Aurora Hills Golf Course on your left. Get on the Highline Canal Trail here. If you don't you'll be stranded on the wrong side of the canal. To reach 12th Avenue, go north on Vaughn (to cross 6th Avenue), and then jog west at 7th Avenue to Ursula Street north to 13th Avenue. Go left on 13th and ride it 2.3 miles to Boston Street. Go left to 12th Avenue and work your way home on 12th to Cheesman Park, a straight shot through Congress Park, along the Botanic Gardens. When you cross Colorado Boulevard at 12th, use the western sidewalk to gain access to 12th on the other side of the road. Follow Williams and Gilpin back to Speer if that's your final destination.

For the Montview Boulevard return, go north on Vaughn (to cross 6th), then jog west at 7th to Ursula north to Colfax. Between 13th and 14th avenues on Vaughn, use the bikes/ pedestrians–only path. At Colfax go west, probably along the ultrawide sidewalk, to Quentin Street, then right. Ride north to Montview along Colonel's Row, then head home on Montview. A detailed description is found in the Colonel's Loop route.

Cherry Creek Trail and Reservoir Loop

Denver
Country Club

Pulaski
Park

Speer Blvd &
Downing St

City of
Brest Park

Leetsdale Dr

GLENDALE

Four Mile
Park

Garland
Park

University Blvd

Santa Fe Dr

Lower Cherry Creek Trail

Confluence and
Commons Park

Blake St

Market St

20th Ave

Auraria Pkwy

15th St

Colfax Ave

Cherry Creek Trail

Broadway

Logan St

Downing St

Cheesman
Park

6th Ave

Speer Blvd &
Downing St

1st Ave

Denver
Country Club

Belleview Ave

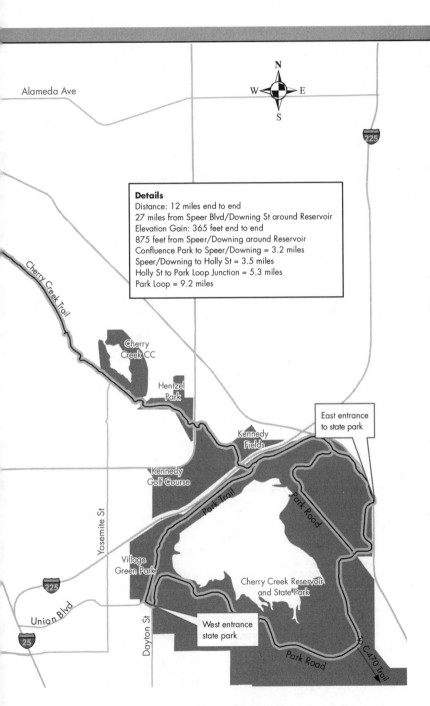

Alameda Ave

N
W   E
S

225

Cherry Creek Trail

Details
Distance: 12 miles end to end
27 miles from Speer Blvd/Downing St around Reservoir
Elevation Gain: 365 feet end to end
875 feet from Speer/Downing around Reservoir
Confluence Park to Speer/Downing = 3.2 miles
Speer/Downing to Holly St = 3.5 miles
Holly St to Park Loop Junction = 5.3 miles
Park Loop = 9.2 miles

Cherry
Creek CC

Hentzel
Park

Kennedy
Fields

East entrance
to state park

Kennedy
Golf Course

Park Trail

Park Road

Yosemite St

225

Village
Green Park

Cherry Creek Reservoir
and State Park

Union Blvd

25

Dayton St

West entrance
state park

Park Road

To C-470 Trail

Cherry Creek Trail and Reservoir Loop

Distance: 12 miles end to end; 17 miles round-trip from Speer Blvd./Downing St. to JFK Golf Course overlook; 27 miles from Speer Blvd./Downing St. around the reservoir; 9 miles around the reservoir

Elevation gain: 365 feet end to end; 875 feet for Reservoir Loop from Speer Blvd./Downing St.

Location: Southeast

Surface: 100% trails and park roads

Route finding: Easy. High water may close short sections of the trail and require you to make at-grade crossings.

Traffic: Cycle traffic is very high on weekends

Direction: Both

Cherry Creek's story is the story of Denver, so it's entirely fitting that we have a trail that follows the creek's course smack-dab through the middle of the city. Denver's earliest beginnings were on the north and south banks of Cherry Creek as argonauts sought to tease out whatever mineral wealth was hidden in the sands of the South Platte River and Cherry Creek. There wasn't much. The real mineral wealth was locked up in the high country, in places like Central City, Leadville, and Silver Plume. Early Denver was flat and treeless. Cherry Creek rarely had water in it, and it was not as deeply channelized as it is today. Early photographs suggest a creek bed just a couple feet below the surrounding land. Some even built "ramshackle frame buildings…on stilts, in the bed of Cherry Creek," according to Stephen Leonard and Tom Noel's *Denver: Mining Camp to Metropolis.* The competing cities of Auraria and Denver consolidated in 1860, but the city did not truly prosper until the arrival of the railroads in 1870. The shallow creek bed periodically permitted major flooding. The first to come after the cities were consolodated, in 1864, flooded Auraria and wiped out the *Rocky Mountain News.* Major floods occurred regularly until the creek was channeled and walled from Downing to Confluence Park. Even these walls proved ineffective. A dam break upstream in Castlewood Canyon in 1933 finally convinced the Army Corps of Engineers to build Cherry Creek Dam, completed in 1950. The dam and the walls are thought to have

stemmed widespread flooding and damage along the corridor surrounding the creek even while rains devastated the banks of the South Platte River in 1965.

The recreational amenity we all take for granted—the concrete path in the bottom of and alongside the main channel—was designed first with maintenance in mind and secondarily for recreation. Even with the improvements, Cherry Creek continues to flood regularly. It drains nearly 25 square miles of metropolitan Denver and, when it rains hard, most of that water ends up in Cherry Creek. Stop and watch the creek sometime during one of those major rain events: the waterline is frequently halfway up the concrete walls. Lesser storms will bury stretches of the trail in 1 to 2 feet of water, leaving behind sand, gravel, and other debris.

Yet for all that, the Cherry Creek Trail and its north–south counterpart, the Platte River Trail, define Denver's urban cycling experience for many people. CCT stretches from the confluence of the South Platte River almost 12 miles to where it connects with the Cherry Creek Reservoir Loop, crossing through a bit of Glendale and a small portion of unincorporated Arapahoe County. CCT is fabulous for a casual ride almost any time and works well for families, but the trail suffers from overuse on the weekends (especially) and is dangerously narrow for high-speed cycling. Limitations aside, CCT provides a great slice of Denver urban life and a critical link to both the major trail corridors of the city and various smaller bike routes. You can reach almost any portion of the city from its many ramps. You'll share it with commuters, students, roller-bladers, runners, dogs, and the homeless, many of whom while away their days under the creek's bridges, in between stints of charitable solicitation at the major intersections of Speer Boulevard.

Start this ride where the Platte meets Cherry Creek. Here sit Confluence Park and the former Forney Museum of Transportation (redeveloped in the 1990s as a flagship REI). In summertime tubers, dogs, hipsters from the nearby Highland neighborhood, and immigrants frolic in the water, mostly ignoring the occasional skull-and-crossbones warnings from the health department about the poor water quality. Kayakers, most of whom have moved on to the cleaner waters of Clear Creek in Golden, fondly labeled the various waves in the park "Hepatitis A," "Hepatitis B," and so on.

Moving east from Confluence Park you'll sometimes see the Greenway Foundation's attempt to mimic Venice in Denver: carefully poled gondolas drifting up and down a set of four locks between Market Street and the confluence. As an effort to reconnect people to a stream that's long been abused, the Venice on the Creek Project is a noble experiment. As an aesthetic experience, well, let's just say that the views are limited and the smells sometimes a tad powerful. It's mostly for tourists, so give them a wave as you go by.

About 5 miles upstream you'll surface like an underground mole and skirt the Denver Country Club along its northern and eastern edges. This stretch is busy, narrow, and on rainy days subject to splash back from the street. At University Boulevard you rejoin the Cherry Creek Trail and wind your way through the Cherry Creek Shopping Center. Good eats and stores abound just a few blocks north.

The last half of the trail takes you out through Glendale, past Four Mile Historic Park, and beyond. You're above ground, there are several parks and golf courses to widen your vista, and you've escaped that walled-in feeling of the central corridor. At Holly Street a new (2009) section of trail goes under the Holly Street Bridge, stretches along the roadless section of the north bank between Holly and Monaco, and then ducks under Monaco to rejoin the trail near Cook Park. This new stretch is a welcome addition to the CCT, as it avoids two dangerous crossings of major streets. You may also be able to see a few remnants of chokecherry bushes, for which the creek is named. At the Iliff Avenue Bridge, water on the path may force you to cross this busy street. Near the Cherry Creek Country Club you can join up with the Highline Canal Trail in either direction. Just before the bridge over Yosemite Street, look for the prairie dog colony on the right. A short climb leads up from

here to an overlook between the Kennedy Golf Course and the ball fields to the northeast. It's a fine place for a drink and a snack. The Cherry Creek Dam looms off to the south, and the park trail beckons.

Continue on to the loop around the reservoir or return as you came. The loop is a great way to extend the creek ride. Drop down from the JFK overlook and follow the trail under I-225. As you climb up out of the creek bed you'll come to a fork. Go either way. Right (west) takes you along the base of the dam to the west entrance of the park; straight ahead (east) brings you to or toward the east entrance. About half of the loop is on the park trail; the balance is on the park road. The park is free to cyclists, and it's hard to get lost here. Much of it is relatively unspoiled in spite of its proximity to several million people. There are still places and moments of extraordinary beauty, especially early-morning views across the reservoir. There's much wildlife evident, and the wetlands on the north are home to scads of birds.

Several options and intersections are worth mentioning. Going east, you encounter a difficult intersection at Cherry Creek Dam Road and Vaughn Way. Use caution here as you cross the dam road. Shortly after, the trail splits again. Most people go right, down toward the reservoir, but it's fun sometimes to ride the perimeter, turning onto the park road at the east entrance. If you go right at the junction, you pass through a section of the park that feels unspoiled; a large group of cottonwood trees nestles along a small creek. Where the trail crosses the park road go left and climb a short hill to the next intersection. Go straight across, then left to stay on the loop road. If you've come in from the east entrance, go left, then left again to stay on the loop road. At the most southeastern point of the park road, a trail crosses with access to Jordan Road (the Dove Valley Loop) and eventually to the C-470 Trail. At the far west side of the loop road go left up a short hill to exit the park, either on the park road or on the trail to the right. You must cross the dam road at the Dayton Street light/intersection to access the trail back along the base of the dam.

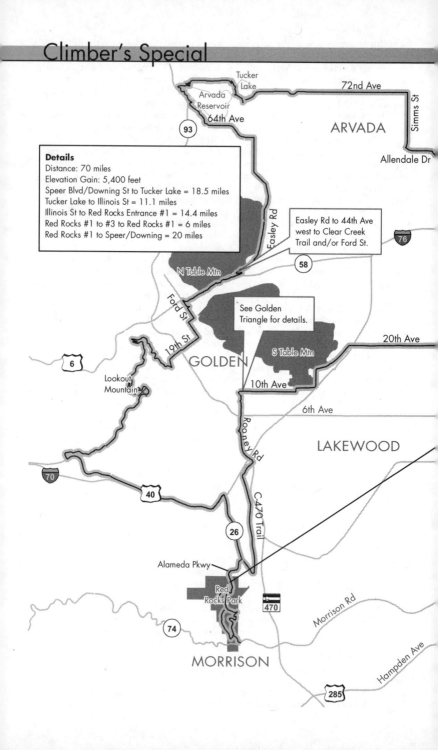

Climber's Special

Tucker Lake

Arvada Reservoir

72nd Ave

ARVADA

64th Ave

Simms St

Allendale Dr

93

Details
Distance: 70 miles
Elevation Gain: 5,400 feet
Speer Blvd/Downing St to Tucker Lake = 18.5 miles
Tucker Lake to Illinois St = 11.1 miles
Illinois St to Red Rocks Entrance #1 = 14.4 miles
Red Rocks #1 to #3 to Red Rocks #1 = 6 miles
Red Rocks #1 to Speer/Downing = 20 miles

Easley Rd

Easley Rd to 44th Ave west to Clear Creek Trail and/or Ford St.

76

58

N Table Mtn

Ford St

19th St

See Golden Triangle for details.

S Table Mtn

20th Ave

6

GOLDEN

10th Ave

Lookout Mountain

6th Ave

Rooney Rd

LAKEWOOD

70

40

C-470 Trail

26

Alameda Pkwy

Red Rocks Park

470

Morrison Rd

74

Hampden Ave

MORRISON

285

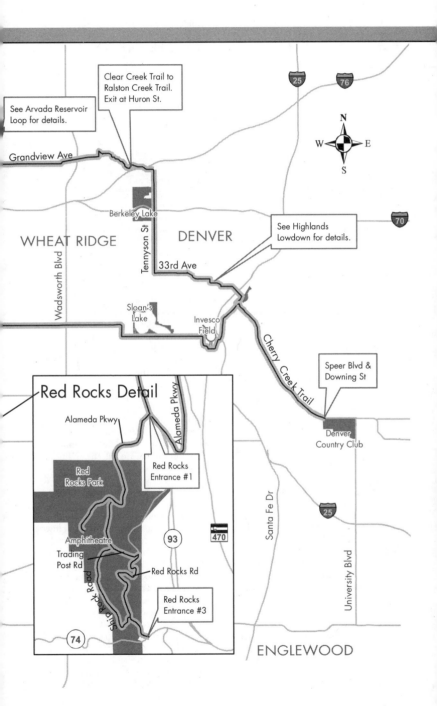

See Arvada Reservoir Loop for details.

Clear Creek Trail to Ralston Creek Trail. Exit at Huron St.

Grandview Ave

Berkeley Lake

WHEAT RIDGE

Wadsworth Blvd

Tennyson St

DENVER

See Highlands Lowdown for details.

33rd Ave

Sloan's Lake

Invesco Field

Cherry Creek Trail

Speer Blvd & Downing St

Denver Country Club

Red Rocks Detail

Alameda Pkwy

Alameda Pkwy

Red Rocks Entrance #1

Red Rocks Park

Amphitheatre

Trading Post Rd

Ship Rock Road

93

470

Red Rocks Rd

Santa Fe Dr

Red Rocks Entrance #3

74

University Blvd

ENGLEWOOD

Climber's Special

Distance: 70 miles
Elevation gain: 5,400 feet
Location: Northwest, west, and southwest
Surface: 90% roads, balance on trails and park roads
Route finding: Advanced
Traffic: Moderate most of the time. Use caution on US 40.
Direction: Both

Colorado summers are littered with charity cycling events and rides, ranging from the Moonlight Classic in Denver (a madcap 10 miles at night through Capitol Hill to benefit Seniors Inc.) to the Triple Bypass (120 miles and more than 10,000 feet of vertical gain), and everything in between, including Ride the Rockies (400 to 500 miles over 6 to 7 days), the Elephant Rock Cycling Festival (100 miles and lesser distances), and the Iron Horse Bicycle Classic in Durango, a race against a narrow gauge train from Durango to Silverton (49 miles and 6,650 feet gained). If you've never considered a ride like this, do it this year. It's an extraordinary sight to look up a hill and see 500 or more cyclists stretched out in a long line in front of you. I rode the Copper Triangle in 2009, an 80-mile loop ride from Copper Mountain through Leadville and Vail with 6,000 feet of climbing, a benefit for the Davis Phinney Foundation. Phinney, the first US rider to win a stage in the Tour de France, developed Parkinson's disease at age 40, and his foundation benefits PD research. To train for the Triangle I cobbled together the Climber's Special. If you've already ridden the Arvada Reservoir, Lookout Mountain, and Red Rocks Park loops, the surprise here will be how easily these rides fit together and the quality of the riding. (Refer to those descriptions for full details of each ride.)

Ride to Arvada and climb to and above the Arvada Reservoir. After descending to 64th Avenue, ride east to Easley Road. Go south on Easley. It winds through rural Jefferson County and cuts southwest along the shoulder of North Table Mountain. Easley is a narrow two-lane road, but speeds are moderate and it's well-traveled by cyclists. At the junction with Hwy. 58, go left to join 44th Avenue. Go right. Either ride 44th into Golden, or pick up the Clear Creek Trail .2 mile past the intersection with Easley. Forty-fourth morphs into 10th Street and carries a lot of truck traffic. Turn left from 10th onto Ford Street. Ride two blocks to 12th Street. Turn left on Illinois Street, which will deliver you to 19th. If on the Clear Creek Trail, make a very sharp left turn downhill into Golden immediately before the Hwy. 58 underpass. Exit the trail at 10th and East streets, and head southwest on 10th to Ford. Make a left. At 12th, go right five blocks to Illinois, then left on Illinois to 19th.

Starting at 19th, climb to the top of Lookout Mountain, then descend Lookout Mountain Road to US 40. Go east and descend a fast 4 miles to the multiple park-and-rides located at the intersection of US 40, Colfax Avenue, and I-70. At the light go south on State Hwy. 26, but use caution, as most cars are getting on or off the interstate. Roll under the interstate and cruise down to Red Rocks Park on Hwy. 26. It's just under 1.5 miles to Entrance #1. Go right. Climb up Alameda Parkway to the highest parking lot on the north side, the Top Circle Lot. Head down halfway, then go right on Trading Post Road. Go right again where it joins Red Rocks Park Road and descend almost to Morrison Road (just short of it there's a wide spot near the Chapel at Red Rocks where you can turn around). Follow Red Rocks Park Road back up to the intersection with Ship Rock Road. Go left, then climb back up to the Upper South Lot—it's steeper than the way you came down. At the top of the climb, where the amphitheater looms above you, go left at Trading Post to retrace your trail back to Hwy. 26.

Cross carefully to stay on Alameda. The stretch here to Rooney Road on the other side of the Hogback is closed to traffic. Enjoy the dinosaur remnants. Climb back up to I-70 on either Rooney or the C-470 Trail. (You must go south [down] from Alameda to catch the trail going up.) Descend Rooney to Colfax. Go right, then immediately left to the 6th Avenue Trail, which sneaks along in the shadow of C-470's concrete. Cross 6th Avenue on the trail, then head north on the trail and/or Johnson Road. At the light near the Jefferson County Sheriff

Railroad tracks in Old Town Arvada.

Department, go right on 10th Avenue.
Ride east on 10th to McIntyre Street.
Turn left and ride to South Golden Road.
Go east to 20th Avenue, using either
Isabell Street and the cyclo-cross option,
or the stealth route through the Denver
West Village Shopping Center. Both
options are shown in the Golden Triangle
map. Once established on 20th, ride east
to Denver, a straight shot of 5 miles.
Just before Sloan's Lake turn right on
Depew Street, then left on 17th Avenue.
Seventeenth is another straight shot east,
to Invesco Field at Mile High Stadium.
Ride around the stadium in either direc-
tion to connect to the South Platte River
Trail just south of Confluence Park. Ride
north, then southeast on the Cherry
Creek Trail to return home.

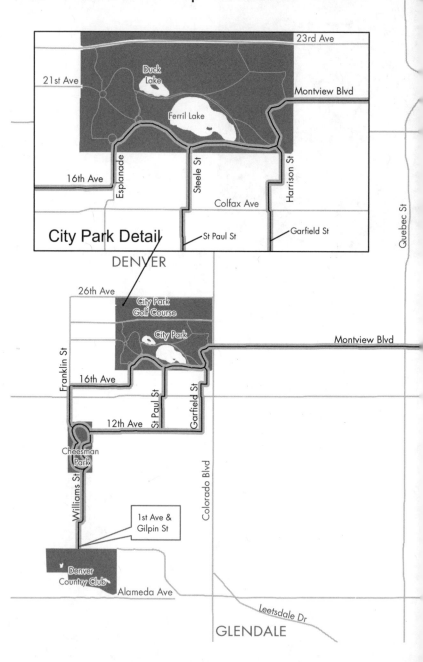

23rd Ave

Duck Lake

21st Ave

Montview Blvd

Ferril Lake

Esplanade

Steele St

Harrison St

16th Ave

Colfax Ave

Quebec St

City Park Detail

St Paul St

Garfield St

DENVER

26th Ave

City Park Golf Course

City Park

Montview Blvd

Franklin St

16th Ave

St Paul St

Garfield St

12th Ave

Colorado Blvd

Cheesman Park

Williams St

1st Ave & Gilpin St

Denver Country Club

Alameda Ave

Leetsdale Dr

GLENDALE

Sand Creek Loop

Fitzsimmons Pkwy

Central Park Blvd

Colonel's Row

Quentin St

Anschutz
Medical Plaza

Colfax Ave

Yosemite St

Peoria St

Use sidewalk on
east and south sides.

Details
Distance: 23 miles (full loop)
Elevation Gain: 600 feet
1st Ave/Gilpin St to Quentin St = 8.8 miles
Anschutz Campus Loop = 2.6 miles
Sand Creek Loop = 2.6 miles

AURORA

Alameda Ave

The Colonel's Loop

Distance: 20 miles out and back; Sand Creek option adds 3 miles
Elevation gain: 600 feet
Location: Northeast
Surface: 100% streets for simple route; Sand Creek option is 100% trails
Route finding: Easy
Traffic: Traffic is never bad on Montview Blvd., though it is a little heavier during rush hour. Use caution and watch for cars on the sidewalk around Fitzsimmons/Anschutz Medical Campus.
Direction: Both

This is one of my favorite short rides in Denver. It takes you out along Montview Boulevard to Children's Hospital and the Anschutz Medical Campus of the University of Colorado. It's perfect for an early-morning spin or a postwork sprint fest. It can be done quickly (in about an hour) or stretched out with the addition of a few extra laps in City Park. And Montview couldn't be a better road to ride on—it's wide, and in Denver there's a striped bicycle lane and a stately 30 mph speed limit. With few traffic lights and no stop signs, this is a great place to work on speed. Crank your heart rate up to 85 percent of your maximum and see how long you can keep it there.

Start at Gilpin Street and 1st Avenue for a change of pace. Work your way north through the Country Club neighborhood to 4th Avenue. If this is your first time riding through Country Club, take time to marvel at the houses of Denver's finest (well, they think so, at least) and enjoy the broad parkways and low traffic volume. Jog east to Williams Street on 4th, then head north across 6th Avenue and you'll soon see the Cheesman Park Esplanade, known to all as Little Cheesman, on your right. Climb up and over Cheesman Park, exit on Franklin Street, and carefully work your way to 16th Avenue. Go right. Cross York and Josephine streets, and then go left immediately onto the gorgeous esplanade in front of East High School. Take a left here, and in a couple blocks you'll enter City Park. Work your way east and slightly north to exit the park on Montview. This is a pleasant stretch through some of central Denver's oldest neighborhoods. Other approaches to the park are also possible. From Cheesman Park go east along 12th Avenue to St. Paul or Garfield Street. Ride north, jogging across Colfax Avenue and entering the park after crossing 17th Avenue—with a light (at Steele Street) or without (at Harrison Street).

The stretch between Colorado Boulevard and the eastern edge of the city, at Yosemite Street, is one of the best around. There's a designated bike lane, light traffic, no stop signs, and stop lights only at the major intersections. The Park Hill neighborhood, located between Colorado and Monaco Parkway, was developed beginning in 1900 and boasts an interesting mix of architecture, including some gorgeous Tudors and many iterations of the Denver square. Across Monaco, you'll be surrounded by the campus of Johnson and Wales University, which offers undergraduate degrees in business, culinary arts, and hospitality. The campus had a short life before that as the University of Denver's College of Law.

Farther east, across Yosemite, you enter Aurora, long the shadowy handmaiden to Denver, but still the third-largest city in Colorado. Awkwardly split between Adams and Arapahoe counties (Colfax is the dividing line), Aurora is known for its connection to a variety of federal military facilities and its hypergrowth in the late 1970s and 1980s. Without a defined downtown business core, the city has sprawled and now encompasses almost 150 square miles of land. It's a place of first and second chances for many.

As you cross from Denver to Aurora, you'll experience that same distinctive Latino flavor found on the west side of Denver: taco stands, *panaderías*, and juice stands, all advertising in Spanish, dot the landscape. At Peoria Street you cross into what's left of Fitzsimmons Army Medical Center. Opened in 1918 as General Army Hospital 21, it became the primary treatment center for the many veterans who had suffered gas attacks during World War I. Renamed in 1920 for the first medical officer to die during the Great War, it achieved national prominence in the 1950s, largely because then president

Dwight D. Eisenhower suffered a heart attack while vacationing in Denver. He was treated at Fitzsimmons, and the rooms where he recovered have been restored and enshrined in that gothic way we seem to have: "Look, Johnnie. Here's where LBJ had his gallbladder taken out; where John Kerry was born; where Nixon had his phlebitis treated." A curious footnote to the whole thing: On the day of his infarction, Eisenhower had sausage, bacon, grits, and hotcakes for breakfast, a burger for lunch, and leg of lamb for dinner. Fortunately, he'd quit his four-pack-a-day cigarette habit ten years before. Go figure. Fitzsimmons was deactivated in 1999, and the inpatient facilities of Anschutz Medical Center, which replaced it, opened in 2004.

You can usually circle the Anschutz Medical Campus in either direction, depending on current construction operations, or wander some of the less-traveled streets to the north. At Fitzsimmons Boulevard (on the north and east) or Colfax (on the south) you'll probably want to use the sidewalk. Use caution: though the sidewalk is plenty wide and there are few pedestrians, bicycles are unexpected and you'll be crossing a number of entrances and exits to the hospital complex, not all at right angles. As you work your way around the hospital, go slowly along Quentin Street to take in the sights. The park at the corner of Quentin and Colfax is General's Park and includes a pond. It was created as a bird sanctuary after the commander of the post was given a couple of ducks. Just beyond, barely visible through the trees, is the commander's former house, and beyond that still are four remaining structures called Colonel's Row, residences for the senior army officers on the base. Finally, on your right, you'll see what's left of the parade ground. Return home along Montview, retracing your path to City Park and beyond.

For the Sand Creek extension, which I highly recommend if you have the time, cross Fitzsimmons at Montview, on the east side of the campus. Find a concrete trail on the other side. Brand new, it works its way north and west to Peoria to a large stand of cottonwood trees, about 1.25 miles one way. This concrete spur to nowhere (for now) traces Toll Gate Creek to its confluence with Sand Creek. Loop around the ponds next to Peoria and head back unless you've got tires to support some dirt-path riding along Sand Creek.

Cook Park Loop

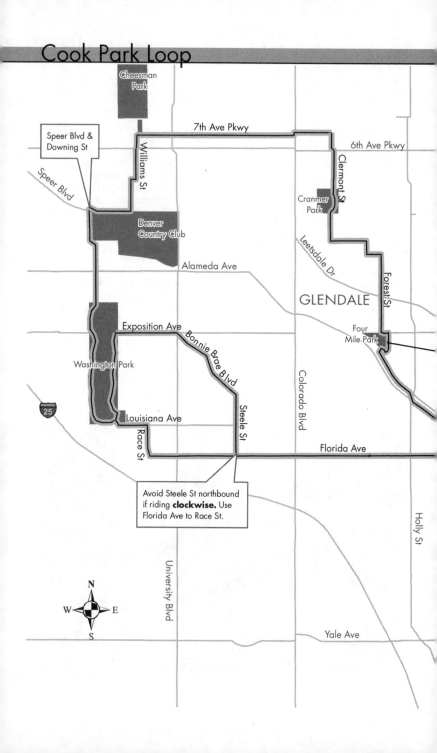

Cheesman Park

Speer Blvd & Downing St

Speer Blvd

Williams St

7th Ave Pkwy

6th Ave Pkwy

Clermont St

Cranmer Park

Denver Country Club

Leetsdale Dr

Alameda Ave

GLENDALE

Forest St

Exposition Ave

Bonnie Brae Blvd

Four Mile Park

Washington Park

25

Louisiana Ave

Steele St

Colorado Blvd

Race St

Florida Ave

Avoid Steele St northbound if riding **clockwise.** Use Florida Ave to Race St.

Holly St

University Blvd

N
W   E
S

Yale Ave

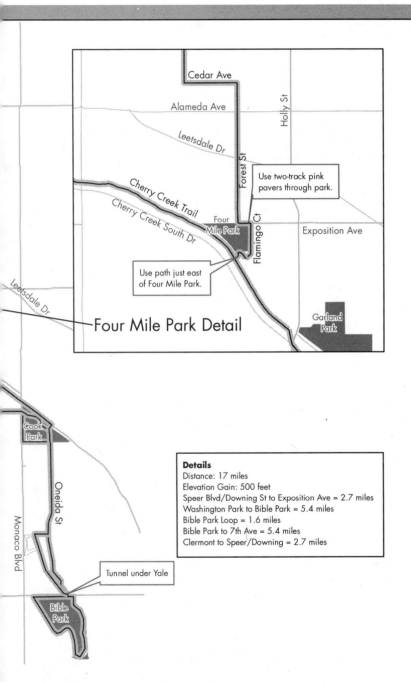

Cedar Ave

Alameda Ave

Holly St

Leetsdale Dr

Forest St

Use two-track pink pavers through park.

Cherry Creek Trail

Cherry Creek South Dr

Four Mile Park

Flamingo Ct

Exposition Ave

Use path just east of Four Mile Park.

Leetsdale Dr

Four Mile Park Detail

Garland Park

Cook Park

Oneida St

Monaco Blvd

Details
Distance: 17 miles
Elevation Gain: 500 feet
Speer Blvd/Downing St to Exposition Ave = 2.7 miles
Washington Park to Bible Park = 5.4 miles
Bible Park Loop = 1.6 miles
Bible Park to 7th Ave = 5.4 miles
Clermont to Speer/Downing = 2.7 miles

Tunnel under Yale

Bible Park

Cook Park Loop

Distance: 17 miles
Elevation gain: 500 feet
Location: Central
Surface: 80% streets
Route finding: Moderate
Traffic: Moderate on Florida Ave. between Colorado Blvd. and Monaco Pkwy.; otherwise light
Direction: Both. If you ride clockwise, skip Steele St. and Bonnie Brae Blvd. in favor of Race St. and Louisiana Ave.

I've always loved the expression "sober as a judge" because I assumed it was meant ironically and sarcastically, a not-so-subtle dig at alcoholic lawyers who left the practice of law for the relatively easier work of being a judge. In the case of Joe Cook, for whom Cook Park was named in 1963, the irony and sarcasm seem out of place. An easterner by birth, Cook came west after World War I and was a reporter for the *Rocky Mountain News* and *The Denver Post* before succumbing to the lure of law school at the Westminster School of Law, predecessor to the University of Denver College of Law. Cook was a district attorney and Denver district court judge for 32 years, and the park honors him for his dedication to the Boy Scouts, Big Brothers, and myriad other service organizations.

This route is one of those shorter in-town choices, perfect for when you're pressed for time but still need to get out. It's mostly flat with two very short climbs: one southbound on Oneida Street and one northbound on Forest Street. Besides passing through the Belcaro and Hilltop neighborhoods, it flirts with Glendale, a small piece of unincorporated Arapahoe County, and passes directly through both Washington and Cook parks. With its mix of street and trail riding, it's a good introduction to urban cycling.

Start at Downing Street and Speer Boulevard, then head south along the bike path/sidewalk to Marion Parkway, the best and easiest way to get to Washington Park. Cross Alameda and Virginia avenues with care, then enter Washington Park heading south—really the only way you can go on a bicycle without running afoul of the compulsory counterclockwise traffic pattern. Loop east and north in the park to exit on Exposition Avenue. Ride east on this narrow street to University Boulevard and catch the light to go diagonally southeast to Bonnie Brae Boulevard. As you wait for the light, look to your right for the misnamed Campus Lounge. Although the connection to DU is tenuous, the lounge remains one of Denver's longtime sports bars, replete with multiple televisions, fish tanks, and decent Mexican food.

As you cruise down Bonnie Brae to Steele Street, you'll pass the small but beautiful Bonnie Brae Park. Go south on Steele past the John Paul II Center for the New Evangelization, home to the Catholic archdiocese and former home of the St. Thomas Seminary. Whatever its politics (the Office of Marriage and Family Life teaches a regular class at JP2C called "God's Plan for a Joy-Filled Marriage"), the archdiocese has been able to maintain a large piece of property in central Denver as open space, and it's a treat to ride by and around. At Florida Avenue, turn left.

Go east on Florida to Monaco Parkway and Cook Park, crossing Colorado Boulevard and Dahlia and Holly streets in quick succession. The crossing at Colorado is the only one that can get a little frenetic. To the north between Holly and Monaco is another mini-neighborhood (part of the larger Virginia Village neighborhood you're riding through) worth exploring. It's dotted with midcentury modern architecture similar to that found in Arapahoe Acres, near Dartmouth and Franklin streets, and in Arapahoe Hills, near Berry Avenue and Lowell Boulevard. At Monaco, cars turn left or right, so position yourself between the two lanes of traffic and go straight across to the path on the other side. It runs both perpendicular to and parallel to Monaco, so go around the park or straight through it to reach Mexico Avenue and Oneida, at the southeast corner of the park.

Climb south up the small hill on Oneida, cross Evans Avenue at the light, and keep riding until just before Yale Avenue and Bible Park. Look right for and join the trail that's below street grade by 10 feet or so. Go left, under Yale, if you want to add another 1.5 miles to your loop; go right if you're ready to head home. The loop around Bible Park is nice enough (if you can ignore the many frost heaves in the trail), and I once saw a herd of goats in a small pen intensively cultivating the park grass, a better alternative sometimes to mechanical means of cutting.

To return, head north from Bible Park along Goldsmith Gulch. The surface here is interesting and may, depending on the outside air temperature, make you feel a little chary about riding on it—it's better than a dirt trail and looks like asphalt, but it's softer and tends to get squishy in the middle of a hot summer day. Soon you'll encounter another one of those Denver oddities: the sunken park at Monaco and Iliff Avenue. It's roughly rectangular and in the shape of an inverted pyramid, 10 to 15 feet deep, and marked by a vigorous stone border. It's actually an overflow detention pond to absorb and mitigate extreme rain events along the gulch. And if you didn't know it by now, this little path would not be a good place to be in a flash flood. A few years back, during a major rainstorm, a Denver police officer tried but failed to rescue a young man caught in a flood at Yale. The man was swept away and never found, either an unfortunate victim of flood or a lucky survivor who didn't want any publicity.

At Iliff go east back to Oneida, then retrace your path through Cook Park. Exit the park to the north, and cross Cherry Creek South Drive. In 2009 the city completed a new stretch of the Cherry Creek Trail between here and Holly. Jump on it and enjoy the ride back to Holly. This stretch leads through a pleasant residential area next to the Cherry Creek Trail and gives you access to the Forest Street bypass, by far the easiest way to cross Leetsdale and Alameda avenues. Just before Four Mile Historic Park, turn right onto a short piece of trail that connects to the end of Vale Drive. Turn left almost immediately on Flamingo Court, on the corner of which there's often parked a faded-teal 1940s-era Plymouth. Go north. At Exposition turn left into Four Mile Historic Park on a short bit of two-track pave. At the cul-de-sac turn right onto Forest and

go north to the light at Leetsdale. Climb the (steep but short) hill to Alameda, cross it, then ride north and east through the Hilltop neighborhood to reach 7th Avenue. From Forest, go west on Cedar Avenue then north on Clermont Street. This will take you through Cranmer Park (a.k.a. Sundial Park, for the large sundial on the west side), named for George Cranmer, Mayor Ben Stapleton's important and influential parks and improvements manager from 1935 to 1947. The park's view to the west is now protected by a view shed ordinance. The neighborhood is an interesting mix of old and new. You can still see the low one-story brick ranches that used to dominate, but many have been pushed aside and leveled in favor of behemoth houses on lots too small for them. The neighborhood was a battleground in the early 1990s between developers who favored scrapes and absurd popped-top conversions and neighborhood preservationists, and it shows today.

When you get to Severn Place and 7th go west. Cross Colorado Boulevard and enjoy the ride along one of Denver's better parkways. Seventh is not necessarily the fastest route, but it's a pleasant, tree-canopied ride through a neighborhood that hasn't suffered the way Hilltop has. At Williams the parkway ends, so go left, cross 6th Avenue, and keep riding south to 4th Avenue. Jog right, then left to Gilpin Street, then south to 1st, bringing you back again to your starting place.

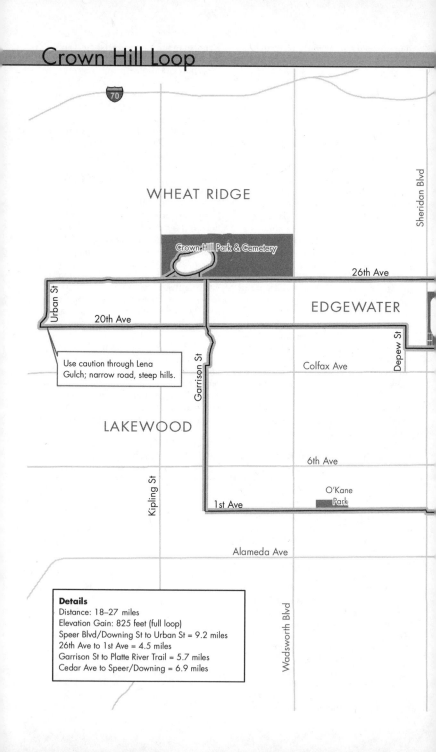

Crown Hill Loop

70

WHEAT RIDGE

Crown Hill Park & Cemetery

Sheridan Blvd

26th Ave

EDGEWATER

Urban St

20th Ave

Depew St

Colfax Ave

Garrison St

Use caution through Lena
Gulch; narrow road, steep hills.

LAKEWOOD

6th Ave

Kipling St

O'Kane
Park

1st Ave

Alameda Ave

Wadsworth Blvd

Details
Distance: 18–27 miles
Elevation Gain: 825 feet (full loop)
Speer Blvd/Downing St to Urban St = 9.2 miles
26th Ave to 1st Ave = 4.5 miles
Garrison St to Platte River Trail = 5.7 miles
Cedar Ave to Speer/Downing = 6.9 miles

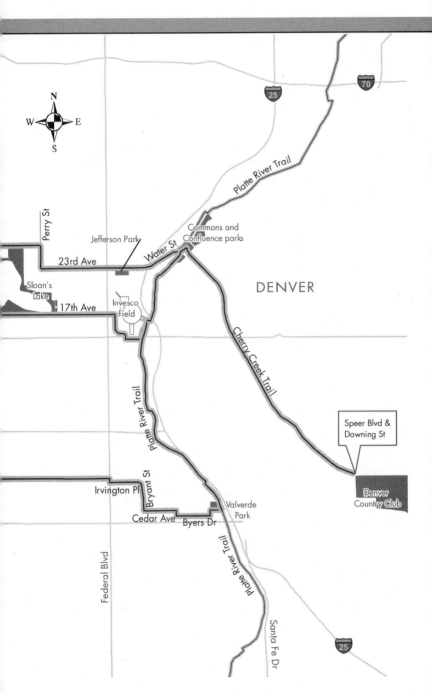

Crown Hill Loop

Distance: 18 to 27 miles
Elevation gain: 825 feet, most of it riding west from the Platte River
Location: Northwest
Surface: Up to 20% trails; balance on streets
Route finding: Moderate. 1st Ave. between Federal Blvd. and the Platte River can be confusing.
Traffic: Moderate most days and times, except during rush hour
Direction: 20th Ave. works best as an eastbound leg, otherwise all directions are possible.

This loop takes you out west along Cherry Creek to Confluence Park, climbs out of the Platte River Valley toward Sloan's Lake, and then to Crown Hill Park and Cemetery along the Lakewood/Wheat Ridge boundary line. Multiple return options exist. Two are shown. One brings you back through Denver's thriving west side. This is a good ride any time of day, but a great ride on weekends and midday, as traffic is heavier during the morning (eastbound) and afternoon (westbound) rush hours.

When Anglos first moved into the Denver area, a number of agricultural regions supplied produce for the fast-growing city, including the land now occupied by Crown Hill Park and Cemetery. It was once part of the Lee brothers' holdings, two English immigrants who correctly saw there was more money in farming in the late 19th century than in mining. Henry Lee, the younger of the two, became parks commissioner of Denver under Mayor Robert Speer but clearly knew the value of land: he sold 180 acres to the newly organized Crown Hill Cemetery Association in 1908 for $48,000 (about $500,000 today). Unfortunately, Henry died in one of the area's first car–pedestrian encounters. The balance of the land eventually became open space, wetlands, and a wildlife sanctuary in the 1980s when Lakewood, Wheat Ridge, and Jefferson County banded together to buy the property and keep it from further development.

Begin on the Cherry Creek Trail heading toward Confluence Park. Cross the Platte River, the low point of the ride, turn left, and exit the trail immediately through the parking lot just upstream of Confluence Park. Ride southwest on Water Street, passing the Downtown Aquarium (formerly Ocean Journey) as you climb up toward I-25. The aquarium was one of the bigger boondoggles of Mayor Wellington Webb's administration. Many couldn't see the point of an aquarium in landlocked Denver, and some were astonished when the fish for the initial collection were stripped from the reefs and seas of Mexico, a weird kind of cross-border snatch that seemed all too culturally predictable. Funded to the tune of $100 million as a nonprofit in 1999, it quickly lapsed into bankruptcy and was sold to the Landry seafood conglomerate. It's a good place for tykes' birthday parties, but eating fish there feels weird, as if you were eating an endangered ibex at a wild game conservation ranch.

Cross the interstate and head west on 23rd Avenue, climbing a long but not steep hill through the Jefferson Park neighborhood. To your left is the park for which the neighborhood is named, a competitor to Washington Park in the 19th century. Farther up to your left sit the remnants of the Baby Doe Matchless Mine and the Chili Pepper, two former restaurants now slated for redevelopment into rental units—a project that both enrages and engages the local neighborhood association. Both Jefferson Park and Sloan's Lake, through which this route goes, are longtime working-class neighborhoods.

After you cross Federal Boulevard, a welcome designated bike lane will carry you out toward Sloan's Lake. Turn north on Perry Street and pick up westbound 26th Avenue. It's reasonably wide and reasonably safe. After Sheridan Boulevard there's a well-marked and well-used bike lane. The route sees regular cycle traffic both from commuters and cyclists bent on reaching Golden and Lookout Mountain to the west. Just after you cross Wadsworth Boulevard, you'll see the cemetery grounds on your right. Keep going. The entrance to the park is just 1 mile farther. If you need a break from the steady climb from the Platte, turn into the park, where you'll find seasonal facilities and shelter. Two major loops circle the park, both concrete. The near one stays close to the lake and is 1.2 miles around. The far one, which leaves the lake loop near the north end, takes you north, west, and south along 32nd Avenue and Kipling Street. The speed limit on the loops is a posted 10 mph.

If you return from here via Garrison Street and 20th Avenue, the total distance is 18 miles. To do that, go south on Garrison, just east of the park entrance, to 20th. Ride west on 20th to Depew Street, go right to 17th Avenue, and ride 17th to Invesco Field at Mile High, which will put you back onto the Platte River Trail. Twentieth is slightly narrower than 26th, but the speeds are slower and there's a bike lane most of the way.

To go farther, ride west on 26th for about 2 miles. After crossing Kipling and Simms streets, you'll be deep into the rural suburbs. Look for Urban Street on your left. It appears just as the designated bike lane ends, but the sign is usually obscured by foliage. Urban drops you down into Lena Gulch. On your right is the Maple Grove Reservoir, more visible at the intersections and in the fall. At 20th turn left and huff your way up the obvious steep hill. Use caution here. Traffic engineers have tried to slow autos by the addition of islands to constrict the flow of traffic, but it always feels like I'm the one being squeezed. This is a good place to ride assertively.

Go right on Garrison and head south and downhill through a pleasant Lakewood neighborhood. After you leave 20th, you enter a Scottish-style neighborhood with ranch homes and curving streets on graceful, wooded lots. Bear right on Glen Ayr, then again on Glen Moor, to cross Colfax Avenue on Garrison. A bike lane will take you 14 blocks south to 1st Avenue, where you turn left. Now you have an interesting and speedy 3-mile stretch ahead of you, much of it downhill. For the most part, the homes in this established section of Lakewood are postwar—low bungalows and Denver squares. The bike lane is well marked, and little traffic will get in your way. Sheridan Avenue marks your return to Denver and into the Barnum West neighborhood. This and the Barnum neighborhood directly east were named for P. T. Barnum, who platted 5,000 lots in the late 19th century, hoping to develop them into a fancy subdivision of Denver. His fanciful dream never panned out, and the area has historically been home to an ethnically diverse working-class population. Although the designated bike lane disappears and is replaced by a parking lane, there's still plenty of room for you and cars in both directions. *Panaderías*, *charcuterías*, and small independent car repair joints predominate. On warm weekends, *ranchera* music booms from the open windows of cars and trucks.

At Federal get ready for some quick action. Turn right and immediately left to Irvington Place. Ride east 2 blocks, then turn south to reach Cedar Avenue. Cedar will return you to the Platte River Trail, but you have to jog .5 block south to Byers Drive (at Tejon Street or before) in order to cross the railroad tracks. From here to Confluence Park it's 3.5 miles, and almost 7 miles to Speer and Downing.

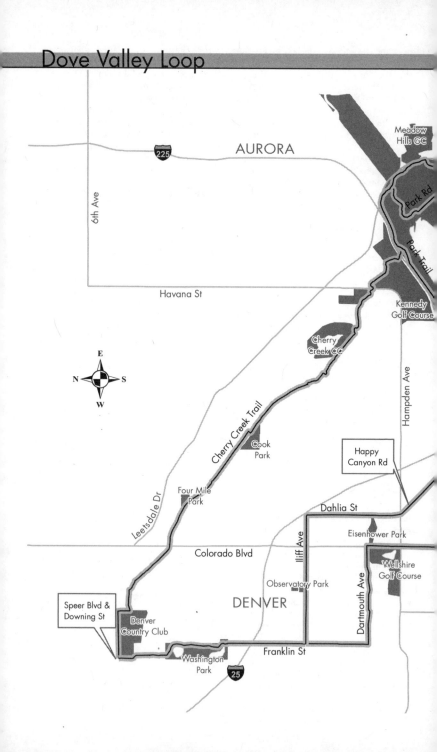

Meadow
Hills GC

AURORA

Park Rd

6th Ave

Park Trail

Havana St

Kennedy
Golf Course

Cherry
Creek CC

Hampden Ave

E

N   S

W

Cherry Creek Trail

Happy
Canyon Rd

Cook
Park

Dahlia St

Four Mile
Park

Eisenhower Park

Leetsdale Dr

Colorado Blvd

Iliff Ave

Wellshire
Golf Course

Observatory Park

DENVER

Dartmouth Ave

Speer Blvd &
Downing St

Denver
Country Club

Franklin St

Washington
Park

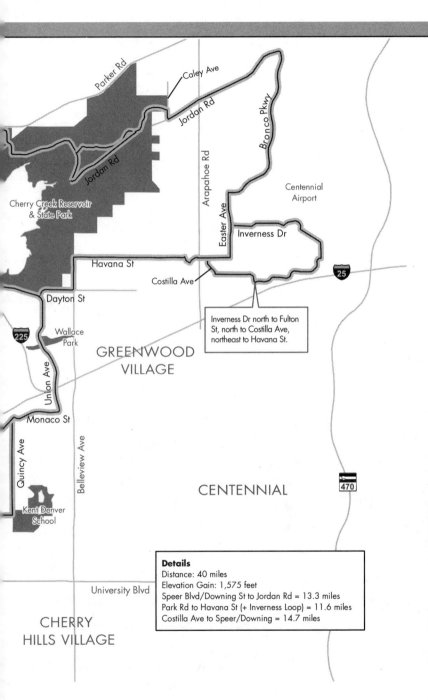

Parker Rd

Caley Ave

Jordan Rd

Bronco Pkwy

Arapahoe Rd

Jordan Rd

Cherry Creek Reservoir
& State Park

Centennial
Airport

Easter Ave

Inverness Dr

Havana St

Costilla Ave

I-25

Dayton St

I-225

Wallace
Park

GREENWOOD
VILLAGE

Union Ave

Monaco St

Quincy Ave

Bellevue Ave

Inverness Dr north to Fulton
St, north to Costilla Ave,
northeast to Havana St.

CENTENNIAL

470

Kent Denver
School

Details
Distance: 40 miles
Elevation Gain: 1,575 feet
Speer Blvd/Downing St to Jordan Rd = 13.3 miles
Park Rd to Havana St (+ Inverness Loop) = 11.6 miles
Costilla Ave to Speer/Downing = 14.7 miles

University Blvd

CHERRY
HILLS VILLAGE

Dove Valley Loop

Distance: 36 miles, with optional 4-mile loop at Inverness Business Park

Elevation gain: 1,575 feet, including the Inverness Park loop

Location: Southeast

Surface: About 40% on trails or in Cherry Creek State Park; balance on streets

Route finding: Moderate

Traffic: On weekends and Bronco Sundays, roads are very quiet. Not recommended during rush hour. Use caution along Jordan Rd., Bronco Pkwy., and Arapahoe Rd.

Direction: For trails, then roads, go clockwise. There are good rolling hills past the reservoir.

This loop is a great way to extend your rides and build stamina once you've conquered Cherry Creek Reservoir. It also features a nice option—to pass by Centennial Airport and loop around Inverness Business Park. On weekends this is a tranquil place of winding roads and rolling hills. Where else can you ride your bike while Learjets take off and land nearby and newbie pilots practice their touch-and-goes?

The route starts with the best of the Cherry Creek Trail and State Park and spins out to where the Denver Broncos practice in the preseason. On Sundays during the regular season, you'll have the roads to yourself. Back in the day (before Invesco Field replaced the old Mile High Stadium), the Broncos did their preseason practice in the August heat in northern Colorado. Reporters and the faithful would trudge north to Greeley in a sort of pilgrimage (hot, suffering, but in ecstasy) to watch grown men slam each other around in ritualized combat. In 2004 the Broncos developed the facility at the corner of Potomac Street and Broncos Parkway for practice and preseason use. It features a mini-stadium from which people can pay to watch the Broncos practice (crazy, isn't it?) and is conveniently close to the Arapahoe County Sheriff's Office and Justice Center, so if the boys or the crowd get out of hand, the slammer is right next door.

Start at Speer Boulevard and Downing Street, or anywhere along the Cherry Creek Trail. Head southeast up the trail all the way to the Kennedy Golf Course, climbing alongside it. After crossing under I-225, ride east around the reservoir. Near the southeast corner of the park, look for a concrete trail that winds southerly through wetlands and

prairie toward a T with Caley Avenue. The trail is 1.2 miles from the intersection where you turned left to descend. You're close when you emerge from the only thicket of trees on the park road. Or go another .5 mile and turn left on a small spur of Jordan Road southeast from the park. This is also the entrance to the gun range, and while there's good shelter from errant bullets as you head out on this spur, remember that most of the drivers in the area have at least two deadly weapons at hand before you flip them off for bad driving. This nice stretch is closed to traffic after .5 mile or so and connects back to the trail just short of Caley. At Caley turn right, then left onto Jordan, and pause for a breath at the traffic lights on Arapahoe. From here it's 1.5 miles on Jordan to Bronco. The surface is good (concrete), and there's plenty of room for you and the cars. Get to it, but be mindful of the fact that you're not in Kansas anymore and that the cell phone–wielding soccer parents behind the wheel of all those SUVs don't necessarily cotton to Lycra-clad cyclists. If you feel intimidated, there's a decent sidewalk along Jordan down to Bronco Parkway.

Turn right on Bronco Parkway and start a great series of rollers to take you west and north to Easter Avenue. You'll pass the Broncos' Dove Valley training complex and Dove Creek (for which the facility is named) at Potomac. Bronco becomes Peoria Street when it straightens out just before Easter. Turn left. As you're cruising along Easter look left to watch planes and small jets taking off from Centennial Airport, then decide if you want to make the optional loop into Inverness Business Park. I highly recommend it. The setting is exceptionally tranquil, the golf course scenery is inviting, and the riding sublime: multiple gentle rollers with nary a car in sight. Turn left at Lima Street, which soon becomes Inverness Drive. Go south, then west, then north again, but always keep to Inverness until you cross Dry Creek Road at a controlled intersection. Go north 1 block on what is now Clinton Street, then right at the small duck pond onto Fulton Street, and north again 2.5 blocks to Costilla Avenue. Ride northeast, then turn left in 2 blocks onto Havana Street, crossing busy Arapahoe Road at the light, as below.

If you're not up for the Inverness Loop, turn right on Havana from Easter and muscle your way north across Arapahoe, certainly on most people's short list for least attractive suburban arterial, but a great place if you need to buy a car, with every major manufacturer represented. The intersection of Arapahoe and Havana is a major one, so use caution. Once it crosses Arapahoe, Havana inexplicably jogs left, right, and left again, before settling down into a fine quiet two-lane plus a convenient lane for cyclists. Ride 2 miles north. Turn left on Belleview Avenue and admire the view back east over the reservoir. A right again on Dayton Street brings you back to the west entrance to Cherry Creek State Park.

If you're pressed for time, the fastest way home is to finish the loop of the park you began 18 miles ago. Cross Union Avenue and head northeast on the park trail until it intersects with the Cherry Creek Trail. Go left to head home. Otherwise, go west along Union through the Denver Tech Center, then north on Monaco Street to the Happy Canyon Road and Quincy Avenue interchange. From here, pick your favorite route home: northwest on Happy Canyon past Thomas Jefferson High School and thence to Dahlia Street and Dartmouth Avenue; or west on Quincy to Colorado Boulevard and then to Dartmouth and north on Franklin Street. You'll wind up in Washington Park either way, a few minutes from where you started. For a full description of these two return options, please see the Cherry Creek Anti-Trail Loop write-up. Also shown on the accompanying map is a short variation along Dahlia and Iliff Avenue, a nice ride back to Franklin passing by Observatory Park and through the University of Denver campus.

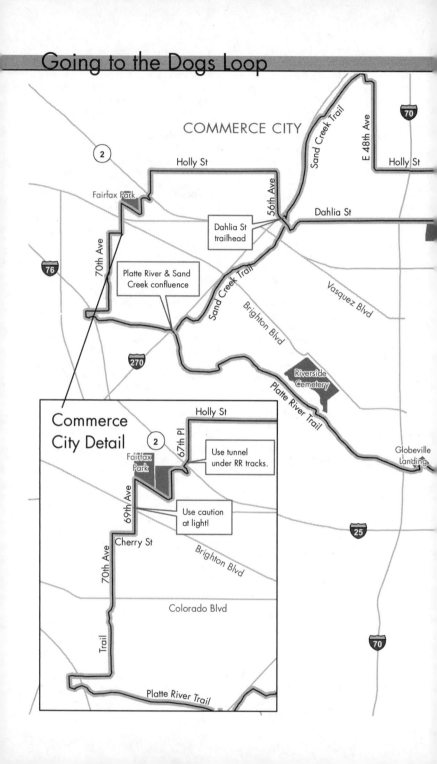

Going to the Dogs Loop

COMMERCE CITY

② Holly St

Fairfax Park

70th Ave

I-76

Sand Creek Trail

E 48th Ave

I-70

Holly St

56th Ave

Dahlia St

Dahlia St trailhead

Platte River & Sand Creek confluence

Sand Creek Trail

Brighton Blvd

Vasquez Blvd

I-270

Riverside Cemetery

Platte River Trail

Globeville Landing

Commerce City Detail

Holly St

② Fairfax Park

67th Pl

Use tunnel under RR tracks.

69th Ave

Use caution at light!

70th Ave

Cherry St

Brighton Blvd

I-25

Trail

Colorado Blvd

I-70

Platte River Trail

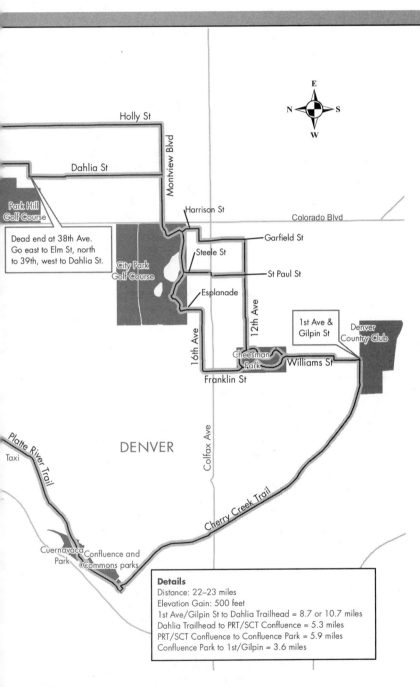

Holly St

Monview Blvd

Dahlia St

E

N — S

W

Park Hill
Golf Course

Harrison St

Colorado Blvd

Dead end at 38th Ave.
Go east to Elm St, north
to 39th, west to Dahlia St.

Garfield St

Steele St

City Park
Golf Course

St Paul St

Esplanade

12th Ave

1st Ave &
Gilpin St

Denver
Country Club

16th Ave

Cheesman
Park

Williams St

Franklin St

Platte River Trail

DENVER

Colfax Ave

Taxi

Cherry Creek Trail

Cuernavaca
Park

Confluence and
Commons parks

Details
Distance: 22–23 miles
Elevation Gain: 500 feet
1st Ave/Gilpin St to Dahlia Trailhead = 8.7 or 10.7 miles
Dahlia Trailhead to PRT/SCT Confluence = 5.3 miles
PRT/SCT Confluence to Confluence Park = 5.9 miles
Confluence Park to 1st/Gilpin = 3.6 miles

Going to the Dogs Loop

Distance: 23 miles; 22 miles if you use the Sand Creek option
Elevation gain: 500 feet
Location: Northeast
Surface: As much as 50% trails; varies with your route option
Route finding: Moderate. Getting through Commerce City can be confusing the first time. Use major caution at 56th Ave. and while crossing Hwy. 85 at 67th Ave.
Traffic: Traffic through Commerce City is very light on weekends, but manageable any time of day.
Direction: Both

I've never actually been to a dog track in my life, but this route is named for the dog track in Commerce City and in honor of the greyhounds that race there. Most lead short, unhappy lives. Huge numbers are euthanized, many inhumanely, in an effort to develop other "winning" dogs quickly. They make great companions if lucky enough to be adopted out of the industry. In my salad days as a private investigator, I found myself one day interviewing a witness in Platteville who rescued greyhounds after they'd been used up at the track. After the interview we visited the dogs. I've had a soft spot for these sweet, gentle animals ever since.

This ride takes in Commerce City, Globeville, and what used to be Adams City, all parts of the metro area few would normally visit. Admittedly, there's not a lot to pull you there. Commerce City long staked its livelihood on the oil and gas industry with the refineries you can see from your car as you zip along I-270. At speed, the area is a blur of huge, intricate towers and bristling pipelines. Up close on a bicycle, the refinery grounds are immense and lonely, especially on weekends. You'll feel sobered and small, not smug, pedaling along on your puny hunk of titanium and carbon. But these kinds of monstrosities are the price we all pay (but especially people in Commerce City and North Denver) for our oil-based civilization. Globeville and the surrounding neighborhoods of Swansea, Elyria, Cole, and Clayton are all within a few miles of at least four EPA Superfund sites. The area has long borne the brunt of the state's extractive industries. Over more than a 100-year span,

ASARCO and its predecessors refined gold, silver, copper, and lead; produced arsenic trioxide for insecticides, medicine, and glass; and left behind a complex and dangerous chemical legacy. The EPA sites are mostly, but certainly not completely, cleaned up. In spite of the area's grimy reputation, new projects like Northfield and Dick's Sporting Goods are luring people north, and the cycling is surprisingly good. And safe. Many of the streets are deliberately wide to accommodate large tractor trailers, and all the people I've encountered while changing flats have been unfailingly helpful and curious.

This is a gritty ride. It takes in all the sights, sounds, and smells of the industrial metro area, including active sand and gravel operations and their futures as gravel pit reclamation sites, animal pens of the National Western Stock Show, a rendering plant, refineries, composting pits, Denver's wastewater treatment plant, truck yards, small office parks, and large manufacturing facilities. And trucks. But I don't mind the big trucks grinding past—they don't go all that fast and truck drivers, in my opinion, go out of their way to avoid coming too close to cyclists, especially when they have enough room (and they do here) to give you a wide berth. Two options are shown on the map: one follows Sand Creek to the South Platte River; the other extends into Commerce City before connecting to the South Platte River Trail.

Start by working your way north and through City Park to arrive on Montview Boulevard going east. Turn north on Dahlia or Holly Street, depending on your destination. If you're headed to Commerce City, stay on Dahlia to 38th Avenue, then jog east 2 blocks, north to 39th, then back to Dahlia. If you're headed to the Sand Creek Trail, use Holly. Either way, watch for railroad tracks in less-than-ideal condition that are not always perpendicular to your route.

For Sand Creek, go north on Holly to 48th Avenue. Pause there to admire the view back to the west. Ride east on 48th. This road is rough, and during the week it's peppered with big trucks, but it's also wide and the drivers mostly friendly. You will pass a Sapp Bros. Truck

Stop just before picking up the Sand Creek Regional Greenway at 49th, right where 49th intersects with the creek.

Sand Creek is a river of unrealized potential. It hasn't had quite as much attention as the South Platte. The Sand Creek Regional Greenway Partnership has done a good job marshaling resources and taking care of the trail, but the creek itself remains a working waterway and a work in progress. It begins out east, and its watershed encompasses about 150 square miles of Arapahoe County. It flows west and north, picking up less-than-pristine runoff from Denver International Airport, the refineries of Commerce City, and the surrounding streets and industrial surfaces. The trail is in good shape and paved, all except for a .25-mile stretch you'll hit just west of the intersection with the South Platte Trail. The unpaved stretch is not at all difficult on a road bike. The Sand Creek route winds and meanders through wetlands overgrown with willows and grasses. If you look closely, you can see remnants of old industrial dams that have been breached, all a reminder of days when we used whatever energy we could harness. Ride the trail northwest to the junction with the South Platte Trail.

If you're headed north on Dahlia, there's a fine stretch of riding between the Park Hill Golf Course and 56th Avenue. Now it's time to pay attention again. At the light turn right on 56th and follow it under I-270, then right again to stay on 56th. Use caution here: the road is narrow, heavily trafficked, and provides a major access point to the interstate. One strategy is to jump the light at 56th if it's clear, then sprint like crazy to get under the overpass and back onto 56th. If you carry the sprint a couple hundred yards up 56th, the road widens considerably and you can catch your breath. Go east .5 mile to Holly, then north.

Ride north on Holly for a ways, then work your way through a quiet neighborhood west to 67th Place. As in *The Wizard of Oz*, pay no attention to those signs directing you to the bicycle route. They'll lead you astray. The dog track sits to the southwest between 62nd and 64th, and it's an easy detour to check it out. There's usually something interesting

to watch on the east side of the track—oftentimes a student-driving course is set up, and for a few months some 3,000 late-model SUVs were parked cheek by jowl, like some prehistoric dinosaur burial ground. Turn left on 67th Place. (It's easy to turn mistakenly at 67th Way. If you do, ride north on Glencoe to 67th Place.) Cross Hwy. 2 at the marked and signed crossing, after which you'll see a tunnel to spirit you under the railroad tracks, a significant barrier here. On the other side, you ride into and along Commerce City's Fairfax Park amid a coterie of prairie dogs that whistle, run, and hide as you approach. Work around the outside of the park to 69th Avenue. Turn left, cross the railroad tracks, and stop at the light. Use caution here—this is a complicated five-way intersection. Wait your turn, then skedaddle west, making sure the oncoming traffic, much of which will be turning across your path, can see you. At Cherry Street jog north 1 block as you pass by Adams City High School. Turn left on 70th Avenue. Go west to Colorado. Cross this major road and keep going straight west. The route is not obvious or signed, but the parking lot–looking piece of ground turns into a short spur of the Platte River Trail and leads you through an interesting gravel operation before crossing the Platte itself.

Turn left on the Platte River Trail. It's not marked and can be confusing since you're also just a stone's throw from the Clear Creek/Platte River confluence and a missed turn here (I've done it) may not be immediately obvious. The route-finding the rest of the way is straightforward. Stay on the trail until you come to Confluence Park and you need to cross the South Platte a final time to access the Cherry Creek Trail. The Platte River Trail crosses back and forth a couple of times as you make your way upriver. Along the way look for the composting operation, the old chute-*cum*-bridge formerly used to herd animals over the river to the slaughterhouses, and Denver's huge wastewater treatment plant. Yep—this is where it all ends up when we flush our toilets.

Soon enough, you'll be back at Confluence Park, from which you can make your way home along the Platte or Cherry Creek trails.

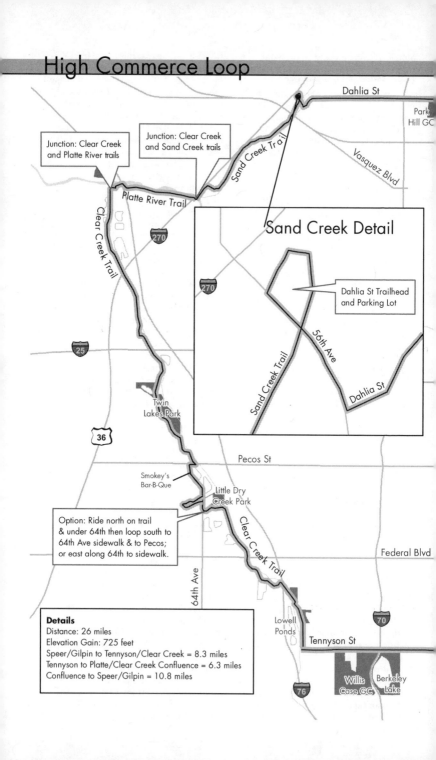

High Commerce Loop

Dahlia St

Park Hill GC

Junction: Clear Creek and Platte River trails

Junction: Clear Creek and Sand Creek trails

Sand Creek Trail

Vasquez Blvd

Platte River Trail

Clear Creek Trail

270

Sand Creek Detail

270

56th Ave

Dahlia St Trailhead and Parking Lot

Sand Creek Trail

Dahlia St

25

Twin Lakes Park

36

Pecos St

Smokey's Bar-B-Que

Little Dry Creek Park

Clear Creek Trail

Federal Blvd

Option: Ride north on trail & under 64th then loop south to 64th Ave sidewalk & to Pecos; or east along 64th to sidewalk.

64th Ave

Lowell Ponds

70

Tennyson St

Details
Distance: 26 miles
Elevation Gain: 725 feet
Speer/Gilpin to Tennyson/Clear Creek = 8.3 miles
Tennyson to Platte/Clear Creek Confluence = 6.3 miles
Confluence to Speer/Gilpin = 10.8 miles

Willis Case GC

Berkeley Lake

76

Distance: 26 miles
Elevation gain: 725 feet
Location: Northeast
Surface: 60% streets; balance on trails—
.25 mile on a good dirt trail
Route finding: Moderate. The Scottish
Highlands area, with its curvy streets,
can be confusing, but getting lost in the
Highlands is not a bad thing.
Traffic: Depending on the time of day and
day of the week, there are tight spots along
Tennyson St. and truck traffic on Dahlia St.
between 56th and 40th Aves.
Direction: Both, but adjust your return
through the Highlands to accommodate
Fairview Pl. and Caithness Pl., both of
which are one-way streets.

The Highlands is the latest Denver
neighborhood to attract the attention
of developers, new urban acolytes, and
people just looking for an affordable
place to live without moving to the suburbs. The original 1858 city was founded
by General William Larimer himself,
when he walked across the Platte and
staked out Highlands as a city independent of Denver and Auraria. The three
were consolidated a year later by territorial decree, and the area became known
as North Denver. The town of Highlands
came into existence in 1885 and included
the smaller burgs of Potter Highlands
and Highland Park. Finally, in 1896,
Denver annexed all of Highlands. Today,
Highlands refers both to the census
area defined by I-25 and Federal, and
38th and 29th avenues, and the three
neighborhoods called Highland, West
Highland, and Berkeley. The area makes
a fascinating ride, as it's chockablock
full of historic districts, interesting restaurants, and small shops reminiscent
of Cherry Creek North 30 years ago.
The High Commerce Loop takes you
out through the Highlands, connects
to Commerce City via the Clear Creek,
South Platte, and Sand Creek trails,
and returns along Dahlia Street and
Montview Boulevard through City and
Cheesman parks.

If you begin along Speer Boulevard,
make your way down Cherry Creek
to Confluence Park. Go north to 16th
Street on the Platte River Trail, 15th
Street, Platte Street, Water Street, or

any combination that works for you,
then cross I-25 on the bridge. (See
the Confusion at the Confluence and
Highlands Lowdown maps for details.)

Cross Central Street and climb the
steep grade up 16th to 30th Avenue, past
Lola restaurant, Olinger Mortuary, and
the Little Man Ice Cream can (you can't
miss them). At Zuni Street make a quick
right, then a quick left on Caithness
Place to enter the old Scottish Highlands
neighborhood, notable for its one-way,
winding streets. It dumps you out on
Clay Street behind North High School.
Go right to reach 32nd Avenue, then
left at 32nd to cross Federal Boulevard
and to circle Highland Park to reach
Fairview Place. Go left. Cross Irving
Street to 33rd Avenue at the next intersection and stay on 33rd to Tennyson
Street, about .75 miles. Go right on
Tennyson. This, of course, is not the only
way to get to Tennyson, and you should
do some exploring on your own, especially on weekends, and especially along
29th and 32nd avenues and up and down
Lowell Boulevard.

Go north on Tennyson and enter
the Berkeley neighborhood when you
cross 38th Avenue. Coffee shops and
small interesting restaurants abound.
Keep going. Pass César Chávez Park
(small) and Berkeley Lake Park (large),
then climb up the hill just east of Willis
Case Golf Course. At 52nd Avenue,
Tennyson jogs right and left as you exit
Denver and enter Adams County. Drop
down the hill to the Clear Creek basin.
Just before the creek, about .5 mile, look
for the Clear Creek Trail. Go right on
the trail and ride it for about 6 miles
toward the confluence with the South
Platte River. This stretch of the Clear
Creek Trail doesn't see a lot of cycle traffic. Southern Adams County along here
is industrialized and pocked with the
remnants of old gravel mines. Even so,
the charm and allure of the trees and
the creek are never entirely lost, and the
gravel mines have created small ponds
and reservoirs along the way, starting
with the Lowell Ponds State Wildlife
Refuge at Tennyson. Just before 64th
Avenue, the trail swings north away
from the creek and curls around Little
Dry Creek, an Adams County park. This

stretch can be confusing but only because the signage is poor. One leg of the trail dies at 64th; the other goes east, then under 64th, and heads north, seemingly away from the direction you want to go. The dead-end option is fine. Get on 64th and ride east across the tracks to rejoin the trail at street level. The north option takes you briefly along the Little Dry Creek Trail before looping back under 64th to rejoin the Clear Creek Trail at street level. Ride alongside 64th east to Pecos Street, where the trail bends south, then ducks under Pecos before resuming its eastward journey. Make a note to yourself to return to Smokey's Bar-B-Que House when you have a chance (on your left just before Pecos).

When you pass under a number of interstates (none are marked), you're getting close to the confluence of Clear Creek and the South Platte. Look for a wooden bridge on your right. Use it to cross south to the South Platte Trail and ride resolutely south about 1 mile, crossing under both I-76 and I-270. Just after I-270, cross the South Platte on the wooden bridge to join the Sand Creek Greenway Trail, the first .25 mile of which is well-packed sand and fine gravel. After that the trail slides along, sandwiched between I-270 on the left and the Suncor refineries on the right. It's still a nice ride, and the Sand Creek Regional Greenway Partnership has done a good job protecting the creek and building the trail. Eventually the trail will join a link from the Stapleton neighborhood and extend to the Highline Canal Trail. Today, however, ride only as far as Dahlia Street, about 1.7 miles from the confluence. A small parking lot and trailhead will be visible on your left, just after an old low-head dam in the creek. Leave the lot at Sand Creek Drive, go left to 56th Avenue, and left again immediately at Dahlia. Heavy trucks travel here, but they shouldn't get in your way—there's a turn lane to Dahlia and it's purposely wide to accommodate you and the traffic. Weekend traffic, of course, is light, but it's safe any time of day. Ride Dahlia south from 56th under I-70, across Smith Road, and along the eastern edge of Park Hill Golf Course to Martin Luther King Jr. Boulevard, a.k.a.

32nd Avenue. Cross the several sets of train tracks through here with caution. Continue south to Montview Boulevard, a slow stretch for the many stop signs and obscured intersections you will encounter.

At Montview, go right and ride west into City Park. Exit the park where you will, at Harrison or Steele streets to return to Cheesman Park via 12th Avenue, or at the Esplanade to return via 16th Avenue and Franklin Street. From Cheesman, finish the ride on Williams Street, down around the Denver Country Club, and return to the Cherry Creek Trail on Gilpin Street.

If you're riding the route counterclockwise and returning through Highlands, turn left on Irving from 33rd Avenue. Ride 1 block north to Highland Park Place and go right, to avoid Fairview Place (one way, west) and to access 32nd Avenue along the southerly edge of Highland Park. From 32nd, turn right on Clay Street, then left on Argyle Place to avoid Caithness Place (one way, west).

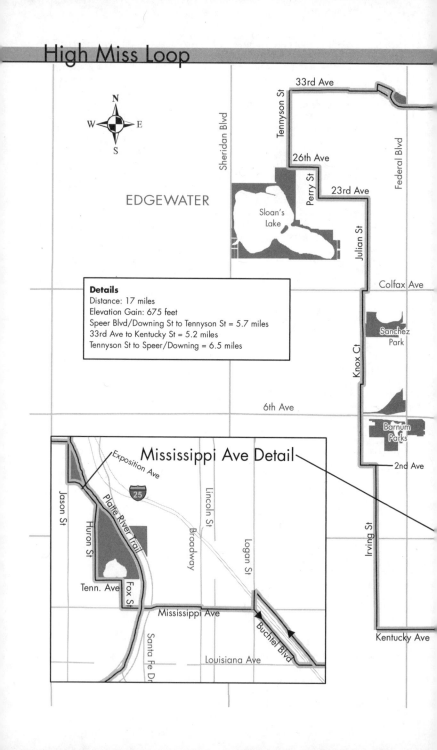

N
W E
S

33rd Ave

Tennyson St

Sheridan Blvd

Federal Blvd

26th Ave

Perry St

23rd Ave

EDGEWATER

Sloan's
Lake

Julian St

Details
Distance: 17 miles
Elevation Gain: 675 feet
Speer Blvd/Downing St to Tennyson St = 5.7 miles
33rd Ave to Kentucky St = 5.2 miles
Tennyson St to Speer/Downing = 6.5 miles

Colfax Ave

Sanchez
Park

Knox Ct

6th Ave

Barnum
Parks

Mississippi Ave Detail

Exposition Ave

25

2nd Ave

Jason St

Platte River Trail

Huron St

Lincoln St

Broadway

Logan St

Irving St

Tenn. Ave

Fox St

Mississippi Ave

Buchtel Blvd

Santa Fe Dr

Louisiana Ave

Kentucky Ave

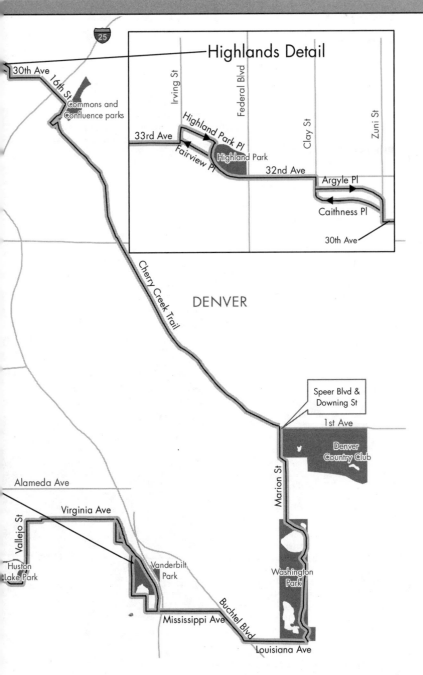

High Miss Loop

Distance: 17 miles
Elevation gain: 675 feet
Location: Northwest
Surface: 85% streets; balance on trails
Route finding: Advanced but interesting. Navigating the Highlands to Tennyson St. can be tricky, and working your way through the stone district along Jason St. can be challenging.
Traffic: Depending on the time of day and day of the week, crossing Santa Fe Dr. on Mississippi Ave. and the short Buchtel Blvd. stretch are challenging.
Direction: Both, but if you ride clockwise, you need to adjust your approach to Mississippi Ave. to take into account Buchtel Blvd.'s one-way status. See the Mississippi Muddle map for details.

This route begins just like the High Commerce Loop, with a trip down to Confluence Park and a climb through the Highlands to Tennyson Street. But where High Commerce goes north, High Miss goes south down Tennyson, to explore the west-side neighborhoods of Villa Park, Barnum, and Westwood. As it works its way back to Washington Park, the route passes through Denver's granite and marble district, acres of stone located along Lipan and Jason streets. The district exists because there's a spur of the railroad that comes down there from the north, and the heavy stone travels most cheaply by railroad. As you cross the South Platte River, you pass by the old Gates Rubber property, a former brownfield turned mixed-used redevelopment project that's currently bogged down by the poor economy. There's good climbing along the way: up to the Highlands and along the low hills of the west side.

If you begin along Speer Boulevard, make your way down Cherry Creek to Confluence Park. Go north to 16th Street on the Platte River Trail, 15th Street, Platte Street, Water Street, or any combination that works for you (see the Confusion at the Confluence map for details), then cross I-25 on the Highland Bridge. Cross Central and climb steeply up 16th to 30th Avenue, past Lola restaurant, Olinger Mortuary, and the Little Man Ice Cream can (you can't miss them). At Zuni Street, make a quick right and quick left on Caithness

Place to enter the old Scottish Highlands neighborhood, notable for its winding one-way streets. It dumps you out on Clay Street behind North High School. Go right to reach 32nd Avenue, then left at 32nd to cross Federal Boulevard and to circle Highland Park to reach Fairview Place. Go left. Cross Irving Street to 33rd Avenue at the next intersection and stay on 33rd to Tennyson, about .75 mile. Go left on Tennyson. This, of course, is not the only way to get to Tennyson, and you should do some exploring on your own, especially on weekends and especially south between 32nd and 26th, and up and down Lowell Boulevard, another bike-friendly road.

Ride south on Tennyson to 26th, then east to Perry and south to 23rd Avenue. Go east to Julian Street and south again another 8 blocks to Colfax. Go right and quickly left to Knox Court. At about 13th Avenue you'll drop down into Sanderson Gulch, along which the

National Velvet by John McEnroe.

west extension of the RTD light-rail will one day run. As a result, there's been a lot of construction along here, but the bike route along Knox has remained open even as auto traffic has been detoured. It's a stout climb up to and across the 6th Avenue freeway, but the descent makes up for it. Go left on 2nd Avenue to Irving and climb again, this time to Alameda Avenue. Ride south through the neighborhoods to Kentucky Avenue. Go left (east), across Federal to Huston Lake Park. Circle the park with a left on Vallejo Street and keep riding north to Virginia Avenue. Go right and drop down to the South Platte River. Cross Jason to pick up the Platte River Trail and ride it south to Mississippi Avenue, or stair-step south and east through the district on Jason, Exposition, Huron, Tennessee, and Fox to Mississippi. This is a sometimes busy light-industrial area that specializes in stone, marble, and granite. The businesses are clustered here because a spur of the railroad runs adjacent to Jason Street. Go left 1 block to Platte River Drive, on the west side of the river. If you've come along the Platte River Trail, exit just past and underneath Mississippi and double back after 20 feet to the southeast corner of Platte River Drive and Mississippi.

This is a major intersection, so be alert for drivers who are not paying attention. The goal is to get across Platte River and Santa Fe drives, then ride east on Mississippi to Broadway. The catch is that Mississippi runs under the main Denver and Rio Grande Western Railroad tracks. And it's narrow. And dark. I like to cross the South Platte River on the sidewalk, pause on the east side of Santa Fe to let eastbound drivers get ahead of me, then sprint down and up the underpass to Broadway. It's not as bad as you might think, though I would recommend you try this route first on a weekend. Yet even at rush hour this stretch of road doesn't carry that much traffic. On the supplemental map for the Mississippi Muddle, you can see this route and a crude but safe sidewalk alternative that spares you the run between Santa Fe and Broadway.

Cross Broadway on Mississippi. Go east to Logan. At the light, bear right onto Buchtel Boulevard and travel .25 mile to where two lanes become one. There, move left and stay left (merging with traffic from an I-25 off-ramp) until you come to the second set of traffic lights at Louisiana Avenue. Go left. Ride to Washington Park along Louisiana, then make your way north through the park to Speer and Downing streets to return to the start of the ride.

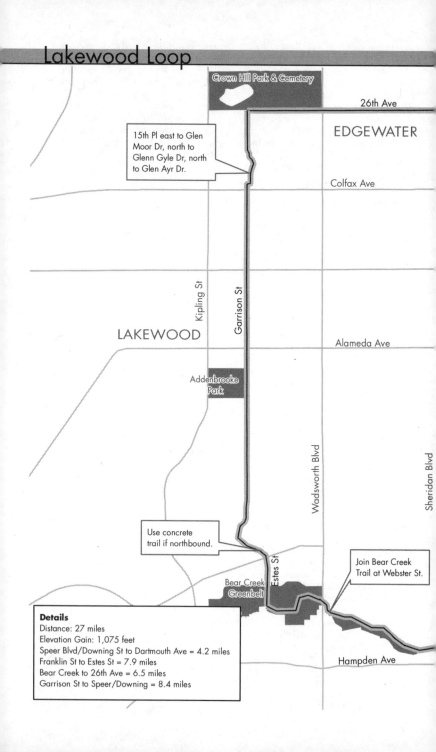

Lakewood Loop

Crown Hill Park & Cemetery

26th Ave

EDGEWATER

15th Pl east to Glen Moor Dr, north to Glenn Gyle Dr, north to Glen Ayr Dr.

Colfax Ave

Kipling St

Garrison St

LAKEWOOD

Alameda Ave

Addenbrooke Park

Wadsworth Blvd

Sheridan Blvd

Use concrete trail if northbound.

Join Bear Creek Trail at Webster St.

Estes St

Bear Creek Greenbelt

Details
Distance: 27 miles
Elevation Gain: 1,075 feet
Speer Blvd/Downing St to Dartmouth Ave = 4.2 miles
Franklin St to Estes St = 7.9 miles
Bear Creek to 26th Ave = 6.5 miles
Garrison St to Speer/Downing = 8.4 miles

Hampden Ave

Perry St crossover

Confluence and Commons parks

Water St

23rd Ave

Sloan's Lake

DENVER

Cherry Creek Trail

6th Ave

Speer Blvd & Downing St

1st Ave

Denver Country Club

Marion Pkwy

Washington Park

Santa Fe Dr

Federal Blvd

Broadway

Franklin St

Dartmouth Ave

Colo Heights Univ

Dartmouth Ave

Irving St south to Girard Ave, west to Lowell Blvd.

Use caution crossing Santa Fe! See Dartmouth Dodge for details.

ENGLEWOOD

Lakewood Loop

Distance: 27 miles

Elevation gain: 1,075 feet, most of it riding west from the Platte River and north from Bear Creek

Location: West

Surface: 75% streets; balance on Cherry Creek and Bear Creek trails

Route finding: Moderate for first-timers; easier if you've ridden the Crown Hill or Red Rocks Park loops

Traffic: Trails have high use on weekends. All the streets have bike lanes, shared-use designation, or are decently wide. Use caution on northbound Garrison St. between Morrison Rd. and Baltic Ave.

Direction: Both

This loop explores a long stretch of Lakewood and shares elements with several other routes, including Crown Hill, Red Rocks Park, and Loretto Heights loops. The distance is right for a fast late-afternoon workout or a more casual weekend saunter. There are decent hills on which to challenge yourself and two fabulous stretches for speed work. The traffic is never too heavy at any time of day, and it's as much fun to ride clockwise as it's counterclockwise. You could, with a little tinkering, do more than 50 percent of this route on the Platte and Bear Creek trails, if you really wanted to. In short, this is a great all-around ride.

Begin at Speer Boulevard and Downing Street. If you're coming from the Country Club area, there's a short stretch of Downing from 3rd Avenue to Speer that runs one-way south. From there, ride south on the Downing bike path. This stretch of Downing has lots of mixed traffic—runners, baby joggers, dogs, roller-bladers, and cyclists—but don't let the distractions interfere with the enjoyment of this ever-so-slight incline past the west end of the Denver Country Club, through which Cherry Creek flows. A friend swears that a slightly demented kayaker in a fit of public access–minded protest once paddled at high water through the country club in his kayak, challenging the startled golfers and groundskeepers to arrest him if they dared. Apocryphal, perhaps, but early Corps of Engineers documents describe an easement through the country club, and it certainly deserves someone like

John Belushi to shake things up. Get off the sidewalk at Bayaud Avenue and enter Washington Park on Marion Parkway, crossing with care both Alameda and Virginia avenues.

Ride counterclockwise through the park and exit at the path and light at Franklin Street and Louisiana Avenue to head south through the University neighborhood, distinguished as much for the couches found on the porches as for the one-story bungalows that predominate. The best of the area is found in Arapahoe Acres, north of Dartmouth Avenue and west of Franklin. A few blocks of geometric midcentury moderns remain. Turn right on Dartmouth, find the bike lane, and proceed west. You're in Englewood now, passing through the northern edge of the city and crossing its mercantile lifeline, Broadway, one of the great streets in the metro area. It stretches from C-470 to the Boulder Turnpike. Much of Broadway around here has changed little in the last 50 years—there are few big-box stores and many small merchants. Within a 4-block area you can find a classic Army and Navy Surplus store, maybe the best electric razor store-*cum*-vacuum cleaner store in the region (who thinks up these combinations, anyway?), a great custom-boot fitter, and a beautiful art deco film theater converted to a nightclub.

After crossing Broadway, you'll soon need to roll the dice at the Dartmouth Dodge, where Dartmouth crosses Santa Fe. (If your timing and chi are right, you can shoot across the intersection without stopping and not get squeezed by the cars trying to snake their way into the single lane of traffic heading west on Dartmouth. For the rest of us, there's the Dartmouth Dodge.) Once you've made it across the Platte River, you'll notice the distinctly industrial feel to the area—but as you huff your way up the hill note the old greenhouse from the 1940s on your left, one of the few still operating close to the city. Top out at Federal Boulevard, then snake your way around the south side of Colorado Heights University, south down Irving Street, then west on Girard Avenue to Lowell Boulevard, where you climb north briefly to Dartmouth again. Go left.

Follow Dartmouth downhill through a small commercial area, cross Sheridan Boulevard, and get on your sprinting shoes. The stretch of Dartmouth between Sheridan and Wadsworth is perfect for speed work and sprints. (Not so the Bear Creek Trail, just a few feet to your left. Where it's not in terrible shape, it winds in and out of picnic areas, children's play areas, family zones, and the like. It's no place for speeding cyclists.) Rejoin the Bear Creek Trail at Webster Street by crossing the creek on a wooden bridge. The trail winds west across an unexpectedly green expanse of bottomland. As far as I can tell, the major ecosystem inhabitants are prairie dogs, cute little buggers that whistle and chuck to each other when danger is around. When you approach a small housing development on your left, leave the Bear Creek Trail on a spur that takes you north across Bear Creek and out onto Estes Street, the beginning of the northbound leg to 26th Avenue. It's about 6.5 miles away.

Estes swings west and turns into Garrison. A nice climb starts at Morrison Road and continues to Jewell Street. This is all Lakewood, an incorporated suburb of Denver since 1959 and still struggling to find its identity. Most of the land now occupied by the city was patented and settled in the mid- and late 19th century by a mix of speculators, miners, and veterans who'd been enticed to enlist or reenlist by promises of 160 acres. Today, Lakewood is home to 150,000, and although it lacks a central downtown, recent efforts by the city and developers show promise in the form of Belmar, a new-urban, mixed-use project with the feel of a real downtown area, and in the form of the nearby Lakewood Cultural Center. Lakewood also boasts the world famous Davie's Chuck Wagon Diner on Colfax Avenue, and is home to the Denver Federal Center, which harbors the largest concentration of federal agencies outside of Washington, DC.

Where the hill starts at Morrison, the road narrows and a concrete trail is available on the right to northbounders. Take it, but be aware that there are two abrupt switchbacks as you climb up from the Bear Creek watershed. After you top out at Jewell, you'll encounter unsurpassed cycling all the way to 26th Avenue. A dedicated bike lane provides a buffer against traffic, and numerous small hills add interest. In a couple of places the road narrows and the lane disappears, but these are aberrations and easy to deal with. After you cross Colfax, you'll pass through an interesting micro-neighborhood known as The Glens of Glen Creighton. Although there's nothing particularly Scottish about the area, its winding streets, oversized lots, and interesting mix of architecture provide a welcome relief to the blander postwar efforts of most of Lakewood.

At 26th, turn right and head back to Denver. There's a designated bike lane most of the way. The portions between lights provide a great chance to stretch out your legs. Go fast. It's about 4 miles from Garrison to Lowell, with a slight downhill gradient to boost you along. After crossing Sheridan, look for Perry Street to jog south down to 23rd Avenue, then to Water Street, Confluence Park, and the Cherry Creek Trail.

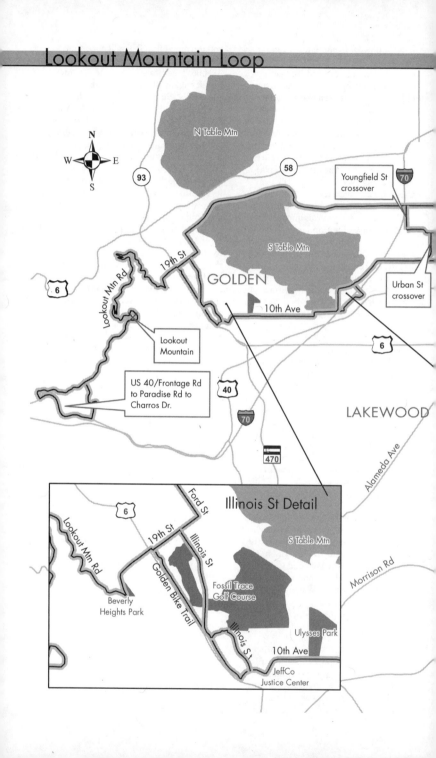

Lookout Mountain Loop

N Table Mtn

93

58

Youngfield St crossover

70

S Table Mtn

Urban St crossover

GOLDEN

6

10th Ave

Lookout Mtn Rd

19th St

6

Lookout Mountain

US 40/Frontage Rd to Paradise Rd to Charros Dr.

40

70

LAKEWOOD

Alameda Ave

470

Illinois St Detail

S Table Mtn

Ford St

6

Lookout Mtn Rd

19th St

Illinois St

Morrison Rd

Golden Bike Trail

Fossil Trace Golf Course

Beverly Heights Park

Illinois St

Ulysses Park

10th Ave

JeffCo Justice Center

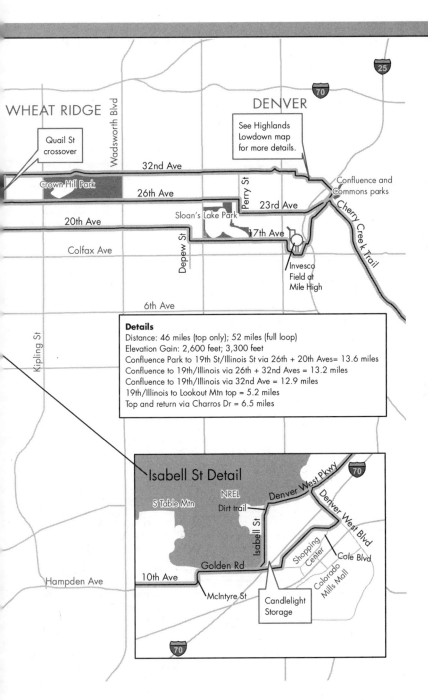

WHEAT RIDGE

Wadsworth Blvd

Quail St
crossover

Crown Hill Park

32nd Ave

26th Ave

20th Ave

Colfax Ave

Kipling St

6th Ave

Depew St

Sloan's Lake Park

Perry St

DENVER

See Highlands
Lowdown map
for more details.

Confluence and
Commons parks

23rd Ave

17th Ave

Invesco
Field at
Mile High

Cherry Creek Trail

Details
Distance: 46 miles (top only); 52 miles (full loop)
Elevation Gain: 2,600 feet; 3,300 feet
Confluence Park to 19th St/Illinois via 26th + 20th Aves= 13.6 miles
Confluence to 19th/Illinois via 26th + 32nd Aves = 13.2 miles
Confluence to 19th/Illinois via 32nd Ave = 12.9 miles
19th/Illinois to Lookout Mtn top = 5.2 miles
Top and return via Charros Dr = 6.5 miles

Isabell St Detail

NREL

S Table Mtn

Dirt trail

Denver West Pkwy

Denver West Blvd

Isabell St

Shopping
Center

Cole Blvd

Golden Rd

Hampden Ave

10th Ave

McIntyre St

Candlelight
Storage

Colorado
Mills Mall

Lookout Mountain Loop

Distance: 46 or 52 miles, depending on route

Elevation gain: 3,000 feet or 3,600 feet, depending on route

Location: West

Surface: 80% streets

Route finding: Moderate. Getting to the base of Lookout Mountain can be the hardest part of the journey.

Traffic: Moderate most times of the day and most days of the week. The climb itself can be exceptionally busy on weekends, when auto/bicycle conflicts blossom. Use caution on US 40.

Direction: Go out on 26th and 20th aves., return on 20th Ave.

Lookout Mountain is one of those iconic destinations in the Denver cycling world. It's close, steep, and challenging. Many people drive to a small park (Beverly Heights) and its convenient parking area near 6th Avenue and make laps to the top, near the Buffalo Bill grave site. An annual race starts here with the record time under 20 minutes. From the park to the top is 4.5 miles and a 1,200-foot elevation gain. The full ride from Denver has everything: a nice warm-up through west Denver and the western suburbs, and a great climb to the top of Lookout Mountain. Many stop at the top, but if you like steep climbs, keep going and make the full loop down to US 40 and back. The distance differential isn't great (6.5 miles), but it adds another 600 vertical feet on a very short shot. As Colorado climbs go, Lookout Mountain is of intermediate difficulty. But don't let that fool you if it's your first time or if the wind is against you as you struggle up the especially steep switchbacks. William F. "Buffalo Bill" Cody is buried here, which makes it a destination for hordes of tourists who are drawn more to his reputation as a western icon and consummate showman than his legacy as a destroyer of Native American bison-based culture. There's a bathroom at the top, with free water from the nice people at the Pahaska Tepee gift lodge. And you'll never be alone. Although the car and cycle traffic don't always mesh well, Lookout is a classic and well worth the trip out.

Golden, the general destination of this loop ride, is a small city west of Denver with its identity firmly intact. It began life in 1858 as a serious challenger to Denver's asserted primacy. Golden's boosters saw it as the natural capital of the state and, indeed, Golden was the territorial capital of both Jefferson and Colorado territories for a brief period, between 1860 and 1867. By 1870 Denver had won the rivalry to connect with the Union Pacific's main line in Cheyenne, thereby becoming the rail hub for the area. Golden prospered in its own right—as a supply center for the mines to the west, as a source for clay and bricks to use as building materials, and as a center for assaying and smelting the ore that poured in from the west. Today Golden is probably best known for the Colorado School of Mines and for MillerCoors (originally Coors Brewing Company), both begun at the same time. In 1873 Adolph Coors started his brewery partnership with Jacob Schueler, and an unsung Episcopal bishop opened the School of Mines, the third of three university-level schools opened in Golden. Both the school and the brewery have prospered and today form the backbone of the city. The school—one of the very best engineering schools in the country—and its campus cover 375 acres west of the main street, Washington Avenue, and south of Clear Creek. At night, to the west, you can see a giant *M* illuminated with LED lights on Mt. Zion. The brewery is nestled down in the riverbed, sandwiched between North and South Table mountains. It offers free tours and free beer, but images of clear spring water derived from years of advertising tend to drift away when you ride close to the operations center and smell the ripe, slightly putrefying smell of the hops used in the brewing process.

Overall, the town has done much to preserve its heritage and protect Clear Creek: It opened a white-water park in 1998 just upstream from Coors, paving the way for similar parks throughout Colorado and the West, much to the chagrin of water lawyers everywhere who see every diversion for recreational purposes as a blow to future development in the state.

Begin at Downing Street and Speer Boulevard. Go west to Confluence

Park and decide how you want to get to Golden. There are three routes to Golden (20th, 26th, and 32nd avenues), and each one has drawbacks. Thirty-second Avenue is the shortest and most direct. It's also the tightest in terms of traffic,

and it takes you through the business side of Coors—including the big trucks, the smells, and a narrow road that actually passes through a portion of one of the buildings. Twenty-sixth Avenue is a very pleasant jaunt as far as it goes, but when it ends, you must elect to drop south (on Urban Street) to 20th Avenue and its pitfalls, or head north (on Youngfield Street) to join 32nd. Twentieth has the lowest traffic volume and the slowest speed limits of the three, but there's a westbound stretch between Cody and Iris streets of about 1 mile without any shoulder, a shallow ditch to your right, and a truly decrepit path beyond to lure the unwary. Eastbound 20th doesn't have the same problem. If you stay away from 32nd, you end up having to do some fancy riding to avoid I-70 and a small nearby shopping center. For each of these routes, the right mind-set helps, as does a good combination of patience and persistence. At some point in your riding career you should check out all three routes and figure out which one you like best.

I like and have mapped here a combination of 26th and 20th avenues, though I recognize the route is a little longer and requires a few more hills. I feel slightly safer here and I like the views: everything from the National Renewable Energy Laboratory and Lookout Mountain to the most famous lighthouse west of Cape Cod and the Taj Mahal–inspired Jefferson County Justice Center.

At Confluence Park cross the river, then go south and out through the parking lot just south and west of Confluence Park to ride southwest on Water Street, away from REI and toward the Denver Aquarium, and what used to be the historic Zang's Brewery, sadly now just another brewpub. Water Street crosses I-25 and curves west, morphing into 23rd Avenue and climbing past Jefferson Park to Federal Boulevard. Go west out to Perry Street, shortly before Sloan's Lake, and go right to join 26th. Keep going west. There's lots of room for you and the cars along here, and a designated bike lane begins at Wadsworth Boulevard. On your right is the Crown Hill Cemetery with its seven-story Tower of Memories mausoleum. Next comes Crown Hill Park, and soon the climbing that began at the South Platte backs off and you have a steady ride for 1.5 miles before you make another turn. Cross Kipling and Simms at the lights and begin to pay attention again. Look for Urban Street. It'll probably surprise you, as the sign is usually covered up by shrubbery and bushes. Turn left. This fun stretch takes you alongside Maple Leaf Reservoir, visible just at the intersections. At 20th, pause.

This intersection is at the bottom of Lena Gulch itself and presents no problem; there's just a short, steep climb up either direction. Sadly, however, the traffic engineers saw fit to try to slow the cars coming down the hill by narrowing and squeezing the road with concrete "traffic calming" islands. What's good for the cars is probably not good for you, so just make sure you have a small lead before you turn right onto 20th and you'll be fine. Cross Youngfield Avenue at the light. Keep going. Twentieth bends south after sneaking under I-70 to become Denver West Parkway. This short section passes through a major office park, so it gets busy at rush hour. Even so, the two lanes give everyone room to play nice, so don't be afraid to claim a full share of the right lane. At the next intersection, where Denver West Boulevard crosses Denver West Parkway, it's decision time again.

Go west, straight across, if you like adventure, don't mind a little cyclo-cross action, and want to see the lighthouse that won the West. This is my preferred route nine times out of ten, and I only

The view from Lookout Mountain.

go left and through the shopping center if it's raining and the track is wet. (The supplemental map The Golden Triangle describes the two routes in detail, but the guide here follows the lighthouse/cyclo-cross option.) Ride confidently west toward NREL. During the George W. Bush years, this skunk works for alternative energy research nearly closed down, but it's found new life under a more receptive administration. Ignore the fact that you cannot go west much farther—the government forbids it and

there's a guardhouse just up the road to keep you in line.

Look ahead and spot the pedestrian crossing sign. It marks a break in the concrete median. Turn left here. There's a steep dirt pitch down through a chain-link fence that leads to a narrow dirt trail atop a small irrigation ditch. The trail is narrow and bumpy, so if it's your first time through, you may want to hop off and reconnoiter. Ride the trail for 100 yards to Isabell Street, and then Isabell south to the lighthouse at Candlelight Storage, one of the best landmarks anyone could ask for.

Go right here, on South Golden Road. If you suddenly begin to feel a little paranoid, don't worry. You've got a Department of Corrections facility on your right, a State Patrol training facility nearby, and a former army installation on both sides. Those antique cannons are definitely not hallucinations. There's traffic here, but it's mostly mitigated by a rarely used center turn lane, so pedal along less than .5 mile to McIntyre Street and go left. A block south takes you to 10th Avenue, a veritable bike highway. It's one-way west, with a dedicated bike lane to boot. Go west without interruption to Ulysses Street, where you climb a steep hill to an eponymous park, then coast down to the light at Johnson Road. Since you'll almost certainly be stopped at the light, look around. Catercorner is the Jefferson County Jail and Sheriff's Office. Slightly higher on the hill is the justice center, opened in the mid-1990s and strongly reminiscent of a certain 17th-century mausoleum. Don't you ever wonder what they were thinking? "Oh, great, the design is perfect. We really want our justice center to remind everyone of a tomb for a dead Mogul empress. That way they'll equate courts with death and will give up any preconceptions they might have about fairness and justice."

Tenth Avenue runs into Jefferson County Parkway. Go right, and right again at the next block to Illinois Street. Illinois winds pleasantly north to the Fossil Trace Golf Course, around which you must make a small detour in order to regain Illinois. Look for the dirt road to your left as you enter the course. Just beyond it, a spur of the 6th Avenue

Trail beckons. Take it, ride out to the 6th Avenue Trail, go right, and right again in 300 feet. The trail morphs into a bumpy road before settling down into a fine stretch through the golf course and neighborhood. Stop when you come to 19th Street.

Nineteenth and Illinois is the start of your Lookout climb, so drink some water and gear down. Ride the first long block west on the path/sidewalk on the right—19th is inexplicably narrow here. A dedicated lane appears shortly before the light at 6th. Keep climbing. You'll pass Beverly Heights Park (with a parking lot and bathrooms), then soon leave the small subdivision behind. When your heart rate allows it, enjoy the views in all directions, watching the hang gliders taking advantage of the thermals and the variety of people and contraptions of all sorts making their way up the mountain. As you climb, cars and faster cyclists will likely pass you—give the cars room, but not at your expense. The road is narrow, there's no shoulder to speak of, and you shouldn't risk a crash to accommodate someone without patience. After an intermediate parking lot, you'll have four more switchbacks and a nice stint in a pine-scented forest, and before long you'll see the entrance to the Buffalo Bill Museum and Grave.

To do the full Lariat Loop, stay on Lookout Mountain Road and enjoy the rollers that lead you to US 40, the frontage road for I-70. Go left and speed down US 40 for about 2.5 miles, then turn left on Paradise Road (the first possible left you can make) to start climbing again. There are many alternate routes back to Lookout Mountain, but I like Paradise to Charros Drive for its steepness. Return to the museum and head down the mountain. Some caution on the descent is warranted. Retrace your steps to 19th, Illinois, Jeffco Parkway, and 10th. Although 10th is one way west for cars, the bike lane allows cycle traffic in both directions. As you make your way east on 10th, use caution at the intersections. Drivers aren't expecting you to arrive from the west and probably won't see you. At Moss Street, in particular, all directions but yours are signed to stop. You, too, should probably stop if there's traffic at the intersection.

After renegotiating Golden Road, Isabell Street, and the cyclo-cross track on Denver West Parkway, get back on 20th and ride it all the way back to Denver. It's a long, fabulous descent with wide streets and/or a bike lane most of the way. Remember the squeeze point at Lena Gulch, and watch for a couple of narrow stretches before you get back to Denver. When you see Sloan's Lake in front of you, look for Depew Street and go right for 3 blocks, then left on 17th Avenue. It'll take you straight back to Invesco Field at Mile High (go either way around the stadium) and then to the Platte River Trail. If you're parched by this point, there's often a vendor selling Gatorade in Confluence Park. The Cherry Creek Trail will return you to Speer and Downing.

1st Ave

Denver Country Club

Speer Blvd & Downing St

DENVER

E

N S

W

Colfax Ave

Cherry Creek Trail

Alameda Ave

25

Confluence and Commons parks

Water St

23rd Ave

Dead end at 2nd Ave

Federal Blvd

Sanchez Park

Barnum Parks

Julian St

Knox Ct

One-half block on Colfax Ave, then left on Julian St.

6th Ave

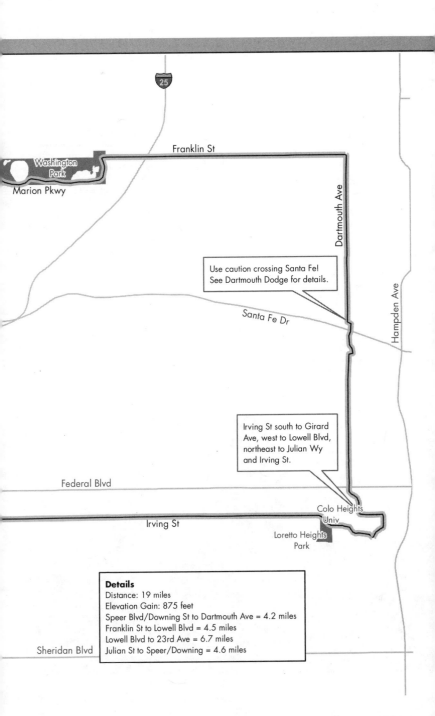

Franklin St

Marion Pkwy

Dartmouth Ave

Hampden Ave

Use caution crossing Santa Fe!
See Dartmouth Dodge for details.

Santa Fe Dr

Irving St south to Girard
Ave, west to Lowell Blvd,
northeast to Julian Wy
and Irving St.

Federal Blvd

Colo Heights
Univ

Irving St

Loretto Heights
Park

Details
Distance: 19 miles
Elevation Gain: 875 feet
Speer Blvd/Downing St to Dartmouth Ave = 4.2 miles
Franklin St to Lowell Blvd = 4.5 miles
Lowell Blvd to 23rd Ave = 6.7 miles
Julian St to Speer/Downing = 4.6 miles

Sheridan Blvd

Loretto Heights Loop

Distance: 19 miles

Elevation gain: 875 feet, most of it during the middle of the ride

Location: Southwest

Surface: 85% surface roads; balance on Cherry Creek Trail

Route finding: Moderate. Navigating the Dartmouth Dodge and working around the Loretto Heights area requires some caution the first few times you do it.

Traffic: Light on the weekends; moderate during the week

Direction: Both

This fine route is a good introduction to the joys of cycling on the west side of Denver. In the right places, the west side offers wide streets, low traffic volume, friendly people, and a variety of rolling hills, something we don't have enough of. The route is also a good way to begin to explore the Dartmouth Avenue corridor, which many of the routes in this guidebook traverse. The highlight and high point of the ride comes as you make your way up Irving Street to Loretto Heights Park. In the process you circle

the former Loretto Heights Academy and College, now known as Colorado Heights University. The school began life as a secondary prep school for Catholic girls in 1891, soon morphed into a four-year women's college, and went bankrupt in 1988, after which its operations were folded into Regis University, up on the north end of town. Bought up by the Teikyo University Group in 1999, the school still dominates the southwestern sky with a prominent bell tower and gorgeous red sandstone buildings scattered over 75 acres at the corner of Dartmouth and Federal Boulevard. The Loretto Heights Loop route mixes flats and hills as it makes its way through the neighborhoods of southwest Denver and rolls through both Washington and Cheesman parks.

If you start at Downing Street and Speer Boulevard, you can warm up as you head south on Downing and Marion Parkway to Washington Park. Work your way through Washington Park—slowly! Once a year or so the Denver police crack down on speeding bicycles; the nominal speed limit is 15

mph. Exit near the southeast corner of the loop, onto Franklin Street near South High School. Franklin crosses I-25 at Buchtel Boulevard, then drifts south through the University of Denver before reaching Dartmouth. At Dartmouth go right. There's a designated bike lane from Franklin almost to Broadway. This stretch can be busy and traffic can be intense, especially at Broadway and Santa Fe. There's not much relief at Broadway, but there's a short piece of trail at Dartmouth and Elati that avoids the light and crunch of cars at Santa Fe. See the Dartmouth Dodge map for details.

From the South Platte River west, Dartmouth is lightly industrialized, but it's a designated bike route and there's enough room for you and the traffic, thanks to a center turn lane. At about 7.5 miles, climb up to CHU, a good climb of about 200 vertical feet. At the Federal Boulevard traffic light, enter the campus. If it's your first time here, make a loop around and admire the setting. The main building, a three-story, red sandstone, Romanesque behemoth, is listed on the National Register of Historic Places and features a fine entry tower that's more than 160 feet tall. The loop around campus is about 1 mile long and well worth it. Exit the campus at Irving, near the southernmost part of the CHU loop road. Go west after 2 blocks to Girard Avenue, then right onto Lowell Boulevard. Go north and climb 2 blocks, then right onto Julian Way, which curves and morphs into Irving. The climb here is again steep and fun. To your right is the back side of the CHU campus, blessedly undeveloped and relatively wild. As the climb tops out, Loretto Heights Park is on your left and, just before Amherst Avenue, a small cemetery for the Sisters of Loretto is on your right.

At Amherst you've entered the Harvey Park neighborhood, and it's a 4-mile straight shot from here to 2nd Avenue. The west side homes tend to be platted on small lots. That pushes kids and families outside to play and congregate in front of their houses. In the summer, *paleteros* walk along and push their carts up and down the streets, hawking popsicles, ice cream, and frozen delights. Traffic is light along Irving nearly all the time, and there are several nice rollers to keep your heart rate up. The major intersections have traffic lights, but otherwise only a few stop signs will slow your ride. At 2nd Avenue, Irving dead-ends at Weir Gulch Park, so jog left to Knox Court and ride north. This stretch carries a little more traffic than the southern portion of the ride, a lot of it driven by the 6th Avenue freeway, so heads-up riding is in order. At 8th Avenue jog right and make a quick left as you coast down the hill to Lakewood Gulch. There's a park stretching left and right here, but more important to note is that the new west-side light-rail project will pass through here, so there are likely to be some disruptions in the coming years as the project rolls out. At the light on Colfax go right, then immediately left to Julian Street, and carry on from there to 23rd. Go right.

Twenty-third runs down past Jefferson Park, crosses I-25, and becomes Water Street, then glides down past the Denver Aquarium and back to Confluence Park. The best way to enter the park and get on the Cherry Creek Trail is from the small parking lot on your right, just before the confluence. Cross the South Platte and you're just a scant 3.25 miles from where you started.

Lowell-Logan Loop to Littleton

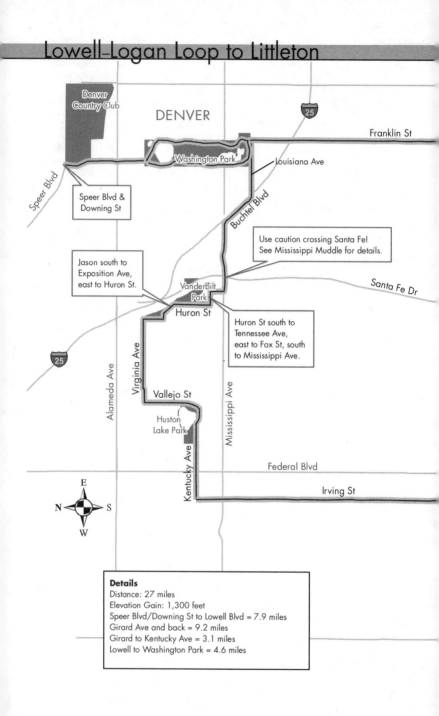

Denver Country Club

DENVER

I-25

Franklin St

Washington Park

Louisiana Ave

Speer Blvd

Speer Blvd & Downing St

Buchtel Blvd

Use caution crossing Santa Fe! See Mississippi Muddle for details.

Jason south to Exposition Ave, east to Huron St.

Santa Fe Dr

Vanderbilt Park

Huron St

Huron St south to Tennessee Ave, east to Fox St, south to Mississippi Ave.

I-25

Alameda Ave

Virginia Ave

Mississippi Ave

Vallejo St

Huston Lake Park

Kentucky Ave

Federal Blvd

Irving St

E
N — S
W

Details
Distance: 27 miles
Elevation Gain: 1,300 feet
Speer Blvd/Downing St to Lowell Blvd = 7.9 miles
Girard Ave and back = 9.2 miles
Girard to Kentucky Ave = 3.1 miles
Lowell to Washington Park = 4.6 miles

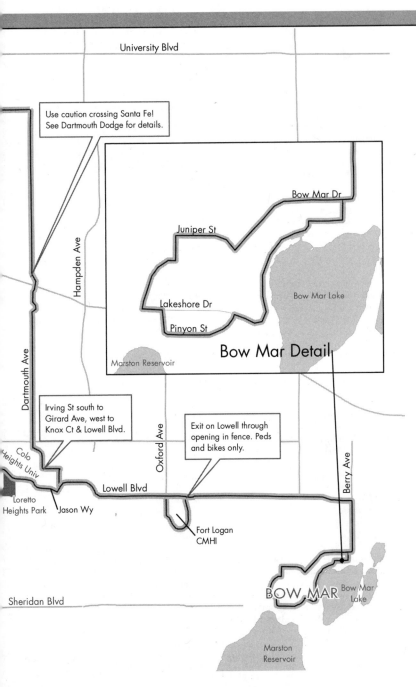

University Blvd

Use caution crossing Santa Fe! See Dartmouth Dodge for details.

Bow Mar Dr

Juniper St

Hampden Ave

Bow Mar Lake

Lakeshore Dr

Pinyon St

Bow Mar Detail

Dartmouth Ave

Marston Reservoir

Irving St south to Girard Ave, west to Knox Ct & Lowell Blvd.

Oxford Ave

Exit on Lowell through opening in fence. Peds and bikes only.

Colo Heights Univ

Berry Ave

Loretto Heights Park

Jason Wy

Lowell Blvd

Fort Logan CMHI

Sheridan Blvd

BOW MAR

Bow Mar Lake

Marston Reservoir

Lowell–Logan Loop to Littleton

Distance: 27 miles
Elevation gain: 1,300 feet
Location: Southwest
Surface: 90% streets
Route finding: Advanced. There are some confusing parts between Lipan St. and Louisiana Ave. on the alternate return—bring your map!
Traffic: Moderate. Use caution on Mississippi Ave. and Buchtel Blvd. between Platte River Dr. and Louisiana Ave.
Direction: Clockwise described for main loop and counterclockwise for Bow Mar loop. The reverse works equally well with suitable adjustments for one-way streets.

This ride takes in two lovely loops in the southwestern part of the city, through Bow Mar, a Littleton subdivision perched among a trio of small reservoirs and lakes, and around Fort Logan, once a US Army base. Federal agencies and installations are scattered far and wide across the metropolitan area. In the Federal Center, we have the largest collection of federal agencies outside Washington, DC. In the recent past the greater metro area had the Rocky Mountain Arsenal (mustard and nerve gas); Rocky Flats (plutonium triggers); Lowry Bombing and Gunnery Range (bombs and intercontinental ballistic missiles); the Fitzsimmons Army Medical Center; and Lowry Air Force Base. Only Buckley Air Force Base remains as an active military facility. One tiny relic of that federal presence is Fort Logan, located at Lowell Boulevard and Oxford Avenue, and once so unimportant in the great scheme of the army that it was called Fort Forgotten.

Created by an act of Congress in 1887, Fort Logan once occupied 340 acres in southwest Denver and functioned over the years as a recruitment and training facility. In 1950 Congress authorized a national cemetery on half of the property, then transferred the balance of the land to Colorado in 1960 for the creation of a state hospital. The state hospital, Colorado Mental Health Institute at Fort Logan, and a variety of drug and alcohol treatment centers now occupy the graceful red brick buildings of the former installation.

Head south from Washington Park on Franklin Street to Dartmouth Avenue. Go west on Dartmouth, across Santa Fe Drive on the Dartmouth Dodge, then climb up to Loretto Heights and Colorado Heights University. The 95,000 white crosses at the cemetery are just visible from the top if you look to the southwest. Drop south to Lowell on Irving Street, then west on Girard Avenue. Go left on Lowell (the name changes to Knox Court for a short stint). Cross Hampden Avenue and begin a slow climb up to Fort Logan. Just after you cross Kenyon Avenue, look west. If you're tall enough, you can see a small number of crosses at the cemetery. Sadly, federal regulations prohibit cycling there. The climb tops out at Oxford Avenue. Go right on Oxford then left on Princeton Circle to make your way around the immense central parade ground. A ring of brick houses, what used to be Officers' Row, looks inward toward the parade grounds. Two-thirds of the way around, at 3742 West Princeton, sits the beautiful Field Officers' Quarters, itself probably worth a separate trip. Continue east back to Lowell. Turn right and ride south on a sketchy stretch of road through a chain-link fence to cross Quincy Avenue. Go south on Lowell for 1.5 miles. This is good riding through suburbia: schools, houses, parks, and small strip malls dot the way. The speed limit is just 25 mph. At Berry Avenue, turn right. There's a traffic light, but the street sign is often obscured by trees and shrubs, so look for Arapaho Hills on your right, a midcentury modern development, as a landmark.

Climb a very steep hill (almost a 12 percent grade) and ride west to Bow Mar Drive. Named for two old-time farm families, Bowles and Marston, the tiny town of Bow Mar sits to the north of Bow Mar Lake and east of the larger Marston Reservoir. Developed in the 1940s and 1950s, the houses are low single-story ranches on large lots. The cycling through the neighborhood is fabulous. Follow Bow Mar north and west until you come to Lakeshore Drive. Turn left and follow it south 1 block. Go right again on Pinyon Drive. If you're tall enough, you can just see the water level of Marston Reservoir. Follow Pinyon to Lakeshore, go right, and you'll be riding along the shore of Bow Mar Lake. Stay on Lakeshore until it returns to Berry, then retrace your route back to Loretto Heights on Lowell, Knox, Girard, and Irving to Dartmouth.

For a more intense ride, return via Mississippi Avenue and Buchtel Boulevard. First climb up Lowell a brief way. Just past Girard (where you turn right to go back to Dartmouth), turn right on Julian Way and keep climbing. Julian morphs into Irving and leads you along the back of Colorado Heights University, with a good view of the old Sisters of Loretto cemetery. Ride north 2.4 miles on Irving to Kentucky Avenue. Go right and head east to one of Denver's best undiscovered parks, Huston Lake. Circle the park with a left on Vallejo Street and keep riding north to Virginia Avenue. Go right and drop down to the South Platte River. Cross Jason to pick up the Platte River Trail and ride it south to Mississippi, or follow Jason, Exposition, Huron, Tennessee, and Fox south and east to Mississippi. This sometimes busy, light-industrial area specializes in stone, marble, and granite. The businesses are clustered here because a spur of the railroad runs right down Lipan Street, and stone, marble, and granite travel best (and cheapest) by train. Go left 1 block on Mississippi to South Platte River Drive. If you've come along the Platte River Trail, exit just past and underneath Mississippi and double back a short way, 20 feet or so.

Pause here for a moment to sort out this major intersection. You need to ride across Platte River and Santa Fe drives, then go east on Mississippi to Broadway and beyond. Two approaches are available. Start by crossing the South Platte River and northbound Santa Fe on the sidewalk and at the crosswalk, respectively. From there you can sprint down and up Mississippi as it passes under the Denver and Rio Grande Western Railroad tracks. Alternatively, cross to the pink sidewalk on the north side of Mississippi and follow it east to Broadway. The intersection is safely navigable at any time of day, but the weekend traffic is considerably

lighter. The Mississippi Muddle map shows both options. If and when the Gates property is redeveloped, the crossing should improve.

Cross Broadway on Mississippi. Ride east to Logan. At the light, bear diagonally right onto Buchtel and travel .25 mile to where two lanes become one. There, move left and stay left (an off-ramp from I-25 will merge from your left) until you come to the second set of traffic lights at Louisiana Avenue. Go left. Return to Washington Park along Louisiana.

Bow Mar Lake.

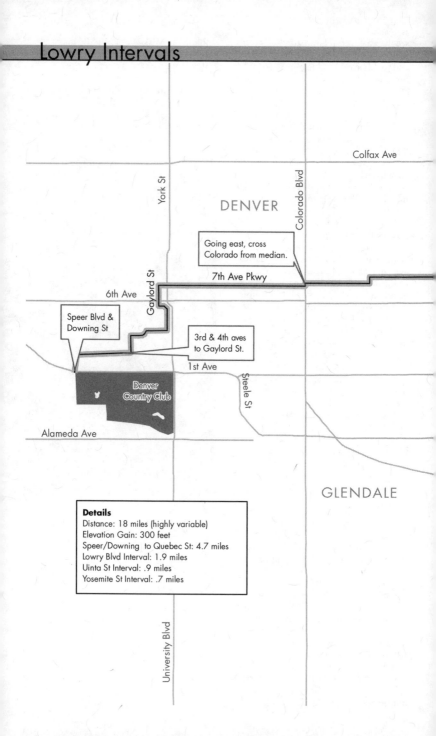

Lowry Intervals

Colfax Ave

York St

DENVER

Colorado Blvd

Going east, cross
Colorado from median.

7th Ave Pkwy

Gaylord St

6th Ave

Speer Blvd &
Downing St

3rd & 4th aves
to Gaylord St.

1st Ave

Steele St

Denver
Country Club

Alameda Ave

GLENDALE

Details
Distance: 18 miles (highly variable)
Elevation Gain: 300 feet
Speer/Downing to Quebec St: 4.7 miles
Lowry Blvd Interval: 1.9 miles
Uinta St Interval: .9 miles
Yosemite St Interval: .7 miles

University Blvd

Distance: 18 miles, but highly variable
Elevation gain: 300 feet
Location: Central
Surface: 100% streets
Route finding: Moderate
Traffic: Light on weekends; busy during rush hour
Direction: N/A

Sometimes you just need to go fast. Blazing fast. To pretend that you're Mark Cavendish, the fastest sprinter on the planet, and you're finishing the Tour de France on the Champs-Élysées with one lap to go, this is the route for you. The heart of it is in the Lowry neighborhood, a recent development that began when the Defense Base Closure and

Lowry opened in 1938 and at its peak covered slightly more than 1,800 acres. Named for a Denver aviator killed in France during World War I, Lieutenant Francis B. Lowry, the base functioned primarily as a training facility. During World War II, bombing crews were trained here and dropped their practice bombs out in Arapahoe County, at the Lowry Bombing and Gunnery Range. During the Cold War of the 1950s and 1960s, Lowry became the first Titan I intercontinental ballistic missile site, with the actual silos and missiles located at the range and the operations located at the airfield. The site was phased out in the mid-1960s, and Denver's missiles were replaced by even bigger missiles

Hangar No. 2.

Realignment Commission recommended that Lowry Air Force Base, which straddled the Denver-Aurora line, be closed. Redevelopment of the site brought with it that rarity of rarities in Denver: roundabouts. Roundabouts mean that you barely have to think about stopping at the major intersections. All you need to do is check for traffic already in the roundabout and go. They're addictive.

located in parts of the country with fewer people around (think Wyoming and North Dakota). Flight operations ended at the same time, and Lowry began its long, slow crawl to obscurity.

With redevelopment in the 1990s came most of the current housing and buildings you'll see as you race around the area. Most of the housing stock is new and relatively undistinguished. A number of original buildings have been preserved for schools, housing, and historic interest. A couple of the huge hangars are still visible as you pedal along. One houses an ice arena, the other an air and space museum that's an interesting chronological survey of Lowry's history and includes a hodgepodge of planes and jets.

The route mapped here begins at Speer Boulevard and Downing Street, then works its way north and east to 7th Avenue through the Country Club neighborhood. Cross Speer. Use the sidewalk to reach the quiet part of Downing to go north from Speer. You'll see it a half block east of the heavily trafficked part of Downing. At 3rd Avenue go right and head east to High Street. Go north to 4th Avenue and then east to Circle Drive and Gaylord Street, to probably the most exclusive of Country Club's four subdivisions. All were platted on a grand scale, but here, in Park Lane Square, the original lots were platted at 18,000 square feet. There are no alleys or sidewalks. Turn north and cross 6th Avenue on Gaylord, then head east on 7th Avenue Parkway and 7th Avenue. The crossing at Colorado Boulevard requires caution. Eastbound 7th Avenue drivers must turn right at Colorado. On a bicycle, turn left onto the median and cross 7th from the median with the light on the marked crosswalk.

Go east on 7th and Severn Place (7th jogs a bit here) until you reach Poplar Street. Turn left on Poplar to 8th Avenue and cross into Lowry on 8th. This approach will bring you to the roundabout at Uinta Way, which roughly aligns with the old north-south runway that stretched from 11th Avenue to Alameda. Lowry Boulevard, the main east-west street through Lowry, aligns with the other former runway. Uinta, Fairmount Drive, and Yosemite Street all intersect with Lowry at roundabouts, so use these legs to add time and distance to your intervals. Lowry, Yosemite, and Fairmount are divided roads with two lanes in each direction, so while there's plenty of room for you and the cars, you have to pick your turnaround spot carefully. Sometimes there's a helpful break in the median, sometimes you just make a U-turn at the intersection. But there's plenty of room to fly. Here's one way of many. Start at Quebec. Go east on Lowry almost to Dayton. Make a U-turn and go west to the roundabout at Yosemite. Ride north almost to 11th, make another U-turn, and return to Lowry. Go west to the Uinta roundabout and north again just shy of 11th. Turn around and return to Lowry and race west back to Quebec for a total distance of about 8 miles, all without a traffic light. Developers are still at work in some of the southeastern parts of Lowry, so there's hope for even more roundabouts and intervals in the near future.

When you're finally tuckered out, head home the way you came. The map also shows an easy exit along Rampart Way, 4th Avenue, and Syracuse Street.

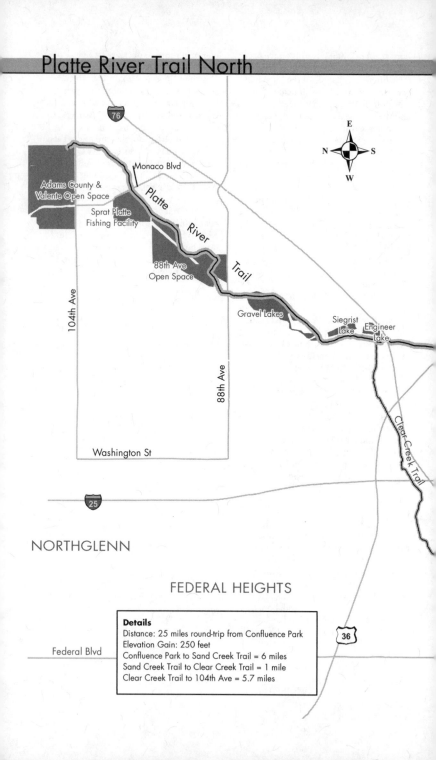

Platte River Trail North

I-76

Monaco Blvd

Adams County & Valente Open Space

Sprat Platte Fishing Facility

Platte River Trail

88th Ave Open Space

104th Ave

Gravel Lakes

Siegrist Lake

Engineer Lake

88th Ave

Clear Creek Trail

Washington St

I-25

NORTHGLENN

FEDERAL HEIGHTS

Details
Distance: 25 miles round-trip from Confluence Park
Elevation Gain: 250 feet
Confluence Park to Sand Creek Trail = 6 miles
Sand Creek Trail to Clear Creek Trail = 1 mile
Clear Creek Trail to 104th Ave = 5.7 miles

36

Federal Blvd

N E S W

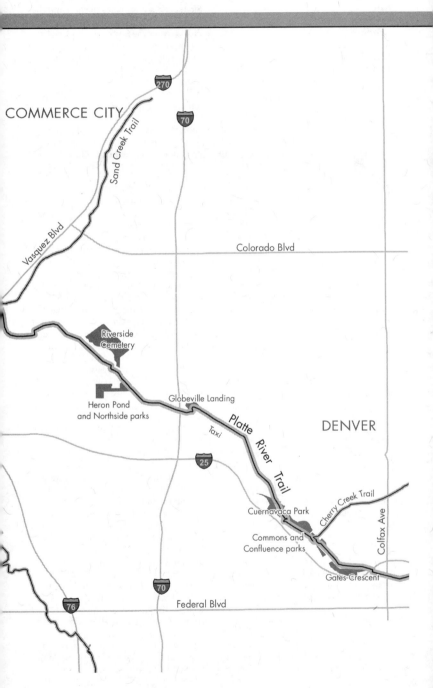

COMMERCE CITY

I-270

I-70

Sand Creek Trail

Vasquez Blvd

Colorado Blvd

Riverside Cemetery

Heron Pond and Northside parks

Globeville Landing

Taxi

Platte River Trail

DENVER

I-25

Cuernavaca Park

Cherry Creek Trail

Commons and Confluence parks

Colfax Ave

Gates Crescent

I-70

I-76

Federal Blvd

Distance: 25 miles
Elevation gain: 250 feet
Location: Northwest
Surface: 100% trail
Route finding: Easy
Traffic: Busy with other cyclists on weekends. One at-grade crossing at Monaco Pkwy.
Direction: N/A

This is a good stretch for an easy and interesting ride with an entirely different character to it than the Platte River Trail South portion of the trail. The south is all parks, golf courses, and suburban housing. The north, or at least the first 6 miles of it, takes you through some of the grittier parts of Denver: past the wastewater treatment plant, the stockyards, and the heavy industry that persists in the Globeville neighborhood. And although I'm a believer in knowing both where your water comes from and where it goes when you're done with it, there's more to this ride than that. The same stretch includes the many new developments north of Confluence Park, including the new Denver Skatepark, as well as the historic 19th Street Bridge, the renovated Pride of the Rockies Flour Mill just north of it, the historic Riverside Cemetery, and the hip Taxi development at 33rd Avenue and Ringsby Court. After crossing under and beyond the Boulder Turnpike, the ride becomes bucolic and you can begin to get a feel for how the South Platte looked before development. Finally, there's much less traffic north than south, and the route takes you to and past the Sand Creek and Clear Creek trails, both featured in other rides in this guide.

Begin at Confluence Park. You may want to refer to the Confusion at the Confluence map to help you navigate north from the park. Once you're across 15th Street on the South Platte Trail, glance left and admire the low office building between 17th and 18th streets. Built in 1865, it once housed a coffin factory and is shaped roughly like a coffin. Just past it, go left up to street level to cross the river on the old 19th Street Bridge, the oldest wrought-iron bridge in the state. Once on the other side, loop back to the right and under the bridge again to gain the east bank of the river. As you do, you'll see the Denver

Skatepark, a great place to check out the latest in urban hipness for the under-15 crowd. After the Skatepark, look right again, across City of Cuernavaca Park, to the Denver Flour Mill Lofts. Once a scary, blighted relic of the early 20th century, it was beautifully renovated by Dana Crawford, the patron saint of, among other places, Larimer Square.

Farther north, on the west bank at about 33rd Avenue, you'll pass by the Taxi development project. The property isn't easy to see from the east bank, so if you're interested, exit at 31st Street and cross over to Ringsby Court on the west bank. What used to be the Yellow Cab garage, repair, and dispatch facility (the 100-foot antenna is still standing) has been converted to a mix of home and office condominiums. Coolness abounds, and there's a great place for a snack or espresso at Fuel Café. At Globeville Landing, cross back over to the west side of the river, then under I-70. A short way farther, look right and notice the bridge to nowhere jutting nearly across the river. Perhaps it's a relic from the days when sheep and cattle moved from stockyards to slaughterhouses, many of which were on this western side of the river. In 1958 more than 2.7 million cattle, calves, sheep, and hogs passed through Denver's stockyards. Nowadays, you'll only see such animals during the National Western Stock Show in January.

Just after 53rd Avenue, cross back over to the east bank. Just beyond you to the east is Riverside Cemetery, Denver's original and historic burial ground, now suffering from a lack of irrigation, though still an interesting place to visit. As you roll north you'll quickly realize that there's water on the left and right. The South Platte River is on your left and the Burlington ditch, a major diversion, is on your right. You'll stay perched here for about 1 mile before the river and ditch bend off in opposite directions. Around the next corner is the massive Metro Wastewater Reclamation District facility. The plant treats wastewater from most of the major municipalities in the area and from 1.4 million people. It treats about 140 million gallons a day, after which the effluent is discharged into the South Platte River. The wastewater district website boasts that for nine months of the year, their discharge of treated water constitutes up to 85 percent of the flow of the river. Your nose will help you decide if this is a good thing or not. The discharge outlets sit just downstream of the plant, after you cross back over to the west side again and just before the confluence with Sand Creek, which, along with its eponymous trail, comes in from the east. Go that way if you're riding the Going to the Dogs Loop.

In another mile you come to the confluence of Clear Creek and the South Platte. Don't get confused here. There's a bridge to your right that crosses the Platte. Ignore it. Bear left and you'll see a bridge that crosses Clear Creek. Go there, cross the creek, and go right to stay on the Platte River Trail. The next 5 miles take you away from the industrial environment. Multiple small ponds dot both sides of the trail, relics of the many gravel mines that supported the earlier development of the metro area. After the street crossing at Monaco Street, trees begin to make a strong recovery and the river itself feels transformed: less channelized, broader, and more like the Platte the early Anglo settlers encountered. In a few short blocks you'll arrive at the end of the paved trail. Here, you'll find the Elaine T. Valente Open Space, 125 acres and a collection of small ponds for fishing and wildlife viewing. Adams County owns and administers the property, and you'll find seasonally open restrooms there as well.

Return to Denver as you came.

Detail, Taxi development.

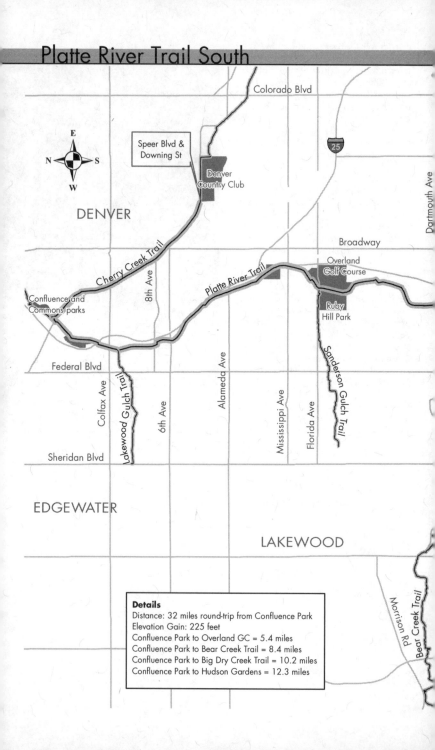

Platte River Trail South

Colorado Blvd

I-25

Speer Blvd & Downing St

Denver Country Club

DENVER

Cherry Creek Trail

8th Ave

Broadway

Overland Golf Course

Platte River Trail

Confluence and Commons parks

Ruby Hill Park

Federal Blvd

Lakewood Gulch Trail

Alameda Ave

Mississippi Ave

Florida Ave

Sanderson Gulch Trail

Colfax Ave

6th Ave

Dartmouth Ave

Sheridan Blvd

EDGEWATER

LAKEWOOD

Morrison Rd

Bear Creek Trail

Details
Distance: 32 miles round-trip from Confluence Park
Elevation Gain: 225 feet
Confluence Park to Overland GC = 5.4 miles
Confluence Park to Bear Creek Trail = 8.4 miles
Confluence Park to Big Dry Creek Trail = 10.2 miles
Confluence Park to Hudson Gardens = 12.3 miles

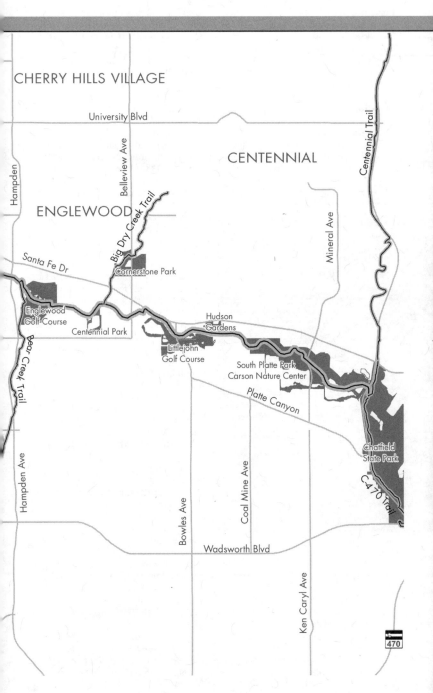

CHERRY HILLS VILLAGE

University Blvd

Hampden

Belleview Ave

CENTENNIAL

ENGLEWOOD

Big Dry Creek Trail

Mineral Ave

Centennial Trail

Santa Fe Dr

Cornerstone Park

Englewood
Golf Course

Bear Creek Trail

Centennial Park

Hudson
Gardens

Littlejohn
Golf Course

South Platte Park
Carson Nature Center

Platte Canyon

Hampden Ave

Chatfield
State Park

C-470 Trail

Bowles Ave

Coal Mine Ave

Wadsworth Blvd

Ken Caryl Ave

470

Platte River Trail South

Distance: 32 miles
Elevation gain: 225 feet
Location: Southwest
Surface: 100% trails
Route finding: Easy
Traffic: Heavy cycle traffic on weekends and during rush hour; moderate the rest of the time
Direction: N/A

Where the Platte River Trail North is industrialized, gritty, urban, and edgy, the trail south, below Mississippi Avenue, is suburban, residential, and riddled with golf courses and small riverside parks. There's some interesting history here, especially within the Denver stretch, but

Near Confluence Park.

after that this is just a pretty ride. Most of the stretch through Denver is slightly tighter than outside of Denver, and you'll encounter lots of people making their way up and down the trail and out to Chatfield State Park to connect with other trail systems (Bear Creek, C-470, and Cherry Creek are the big ones). Children and families abound on the

weekends, so slow down and pass carefully. The ride takes you past the Bear Creek and Big Dry Creek trails, both featured in other rides.

Start at Confluence Park and head south. There are trails on both sides of the South Platte, but stay on the east bank. There's less traffic and none of the rough bridges that you'll find on the west bank. Centennial Gardens and Elitch Gardens now occupy space that used to be a consolidated marshaling yard for the railroads. In the late 1970s and early 1980s, the homeless had a huge camp under the massive Speer viaduct and runners could skirt it on their way through the mostly empty railroad area. Redevelopment under former Denver mayor Federico Peña changed all that, and now we have the Pepsi Center, Elitch Gardens, and Centennial Gardens instead. In 2009 the Greenway Foundation sponsored a planning process for the river south of Confluence Park. Among the ideas under consideration is to use the land under Elitch and Centennial gardens to create an international-quality white-water competition course. When the east bank trail ends at Invesco Field, cross over the South Platte and continue on the west side. At 14th Avenue, there'll soon be a new bridge that will carry the Regional Transportation District's light-rail out along the west corridor, roughly along the existing Lakewood Dry Gulch Trail to Golden. When the work is completed, sometime in 2013, the trail should be much improved from its current neglected and disrupted state.

At 13th Avenue you'll encounter a rare at-grade crossing on the trail. Just beyond it is Excel's Zuni Street power plant, a mid-20th-century behemoth that sucks 98 million gallons of water from the river for cooling each year. Plans are afoot either to close the plant entirely or to replace the fabric dam you see with a simpler closed-loop cooling system that would allow for the removal of the ugly dam, one of the last dangerous obstacles on the river.

Moving south, the stretch between 8th Avenue and Mississippi is probably the most industrialized you'll pass through, with I-25 and Santa Fe just beyond the trail. Rezoning and redevelopment will continue to change the face of these neighborhoods and the river corridor in the years to come. When traffic is backed up here, it's a pleasure to watch the drivers stew as you zip by. Farther south still, Overland Golf Course had a rich history as a horse track, an auto racing track, and an airfield before being purchased by Denver in 1918. Exit the Platte Trail at Florida Avenue and go west if you want to explore the Sanderson Gulch Trail. Stretches of it are in disrepair, but it winds a little more than 3 miles through a series of connected parks to Denver's western edge. Barely visible to the west is Ruby Hill, where generations of kids have launched sleds and toboggans after big snowstorms. Today, the City of Denver and Winter Park Resort sponsor a winter terrain park on Ruby Hill for snowboarders and skiers who can't make it to the mountains.

Below Dartmouth Avenue you'll soon run into a brownfield development in Sheridan called River Point. Although it has all the usual big-box stores, the development also brought with it a short stretch of new trail and a new bridge at the confluence with Bear Creek. Just beyond the bridge is the Englewood Municipal Golf Course; it's the site of a former landfill. At Union Avenue a series of breached low-head dams provide an early spring playground for kayakers, who flock here like salmon to surf, spin, and flip in the waves. Seasonally at the park you'll find water and toilets, if you need them. Just south of Union, the Big Dry Creek Trail enters from the east. As you move into Littleton, the water in the river gets cleaner and the scenery is more inviting. Between Bowles and C-470, a series of parks and ponds lend this section a bucolic feel. Multiple small drops in the river give aspiring canoeists and tubers a 3-mile stretch in which to float and practice their ferry moves. Golf courses and nurseries abound.

Finally, just before reaching C-470, you'll come upon the last free auto access point before entering Chatfield State Park. A small parking lot gives access to the river, the trail, and the fishing ponds next door. Just south of C-470, you'll come to the end of the Platte River Trail.

It joins here with the C-470 Trail (heading west) and the Centennial Trail (heading east).

Return to Denver as you came.

Near Union Chutes.

Red Rocks Park Loop

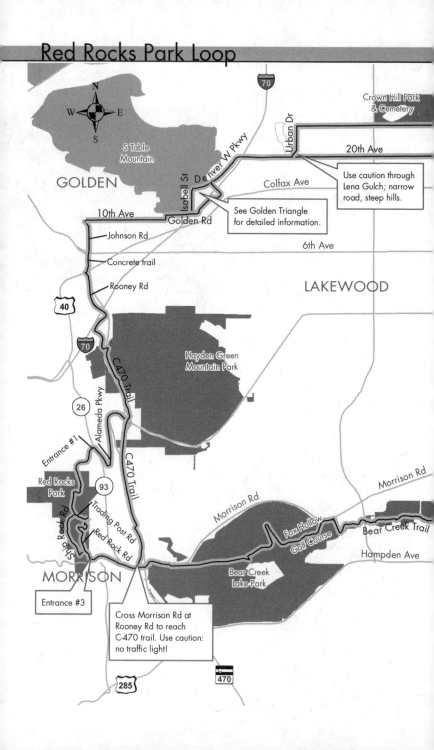

N
W E
S

I-70

Crown Hill Park
& Cemetery

Urban Dr

20th Ave

S Table
Mountain

GOLDEN

Isabell St

Denver W Pkwy

Colfax Ave

Use caution through
Lena Gulch; narrow
road, steep hills.

10th Ave

Golden Rd

See Golden Triangle
for detailed information.

Johnson Rd

6th Ave

Concrete trail

LAKEWOOD

Rooney Rd

US 40

I-70

Hayden Green
Mountain Park

C470 Trail

Alameda Pkwy

26

Entrance #1

C470 Trail

93

Red Rocks
Park

Morrison Rd

Trading Post Rd

Morrison Rd

Fox Hollow
Golf Course

Bear Creek Trail

Ship Rock Rd

Red Rock Rd

Hampden Ave

MORRISON

Bear Creek
Lake Park

Entrance #3

Cross Morrison Rd at
Rooney Rd to reach
C-470 trail. Use caution:
no traffic light!

US 285

I-470

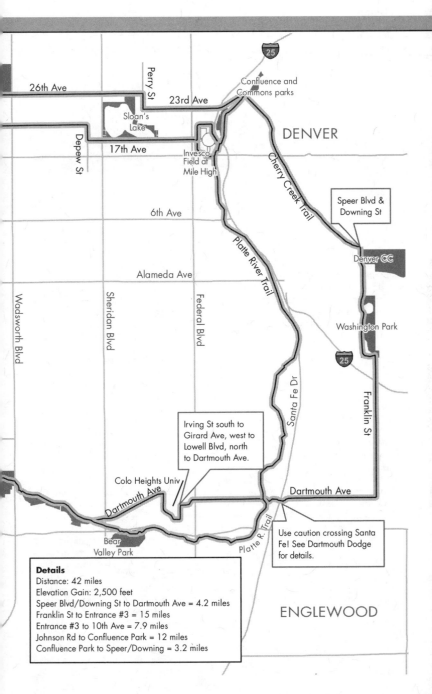

26th Ave

Perry St

Confluence and
Commons parks

23rd Ave

Sloan's
Lake

DENVER

17th Ave

Depew St

Invesco
Field at
Mile High

Cherry Creek Trail

Speer Blvd &
Downing St

6th Ave

Denver CC

Platte River Trail

Alameda Ave

Wadsworth Blvd

Sheridan Blvd

Federal Blvd

Washington Park

25

Santa Fe Dr

Franklin St

Irving St south to
Girard Ave, west to
Lowell Blvd, north
to Dartmouth Ave.

Colo Heights Univ

Dartmouth Ave

Dartmouth Ave

Bear
Valley Park

Platte R. Trail

Use caution crossing Santa
Fe! See Dartmouth Dodge
for details.

Details
Distance: 42 miles
Elevation Gain: 2,500 feet
Speer Blvd/Downing St to Dartmouth Ave = 4.2 miles
Franklin St to Entrance #3 = 15 miles
Entrance #3 to 10th Ave = 7.9 miles
Johnson Rd to Confluence Park = 12 miles
Confluence Park to Speer/Downing = 3.2 miles

ENGLEWOOD

Red Rocks Park Loop

Distance: 42 miles; several variations possible

Elevation gain: 2,500 feet

Location: Southwest

Surface: 50% to 75% trails; balance on streets

Route finding: Moderate. Use caution through the Golden Triangle.

Traffic: Moderate on weekends. Use caution along S. Golden Rd., Golden West Blvd., and 20th Ave. at Lena Gulch.

Direction: Clockwise (south, then west up Bear Creek) makes for a steep climb into Red Rocks. Counterclockwise (west from Confluence Park) makes for a fabulous descent into Bear Creek if you don't want a big climb up to Red Rocks.

This is one of the best longer rides in the greater metro area. Using mostly streets or as much as 75 percent trails, it takes in Washington Park and the Bear Creek system to launch you west to Red Rocks Park, one of the great destinations in the area. There, you climb steeply through slabs of Fountain Formation sandstone, a stunning backdrop to your ride that helps distract you from the steep, but mercifully short, climb. The City of Denver bought the property in 1926, developed it with help from the Civilian Conservation Corps during the Great Depression, and dedicated the amphitheater in 1941. It now serves as a spectacular site for rock concerts and a famous Easter Sunday sunrise service. Leaving Red Rocks, you scoot through the fossilized bones and footprints of Dinosaur Ridge just east of the park along Alameda Parkway, closed to automobile traffic between Hwy. 93 and Rooney Road. After joining the C-470 Trail, the ride peaks out near Green Mountain, descends the 6th Avenue Trail, then works its way back to Denver on surface streets. If you ride this clockwise and skip the climb into Red Rocks, the descent on Rooney Road or the C-470 Trail is fast, smooth, and not to be missed.

If you plan to ride the trails as much as possible, start at Confluence Park. Ride south 8.5 miles on the Platte River Trail to the confluence with Bear Creek. Just before the confluence you'll pass under Hampden Avenue (US 285). Go west along the winding Bear Creek Trail 4.2 miles to and through Bear

Creek Park. For everyone else, start at Speer Boulevard and Downing Street. Ride south through Washington Park on Marion Parkway and continue south on Franklin Street to Dartmouth Avenue. Go west to cross Santa Fe Drive, using the Dartmouth Dodge to avoid the worst of the traffic there. (See the supplemental map for details.) Climb to Loretto Heights, as in the Lakewood Loop, and work your way south and west around the Colorado Heights University campus on Irving Street and Girard Avenue to Dartmouth. Continue west across Sheridan to join the Bear Creek Trail at Webster Street. You'll have a great ride up to CHU and avoid most of the unpleasant and crowded areas along the early sections of the Bear Creek Trail.

Whether you've followed the trails or streets, the directions converge on the Bear Creek Trail at Webster and Dartmouth. Go west up the Bear Creek drainage, one of several major tributaries of the Platte River that tumble out of the mountains (the others are Clear Creek, Boulder Creek, and the Cache La Poudre). The trail snakes in and out of towering cottonwoods and makes for a nice ride, dappled with sunlight and cooler temperatures in the shade, but it's not a great place to go fast (especially on weekends when the trail is more crowded), as there are a number of sharp, dangerous corners. There are several sublime stretches, including a short stint through a meadow with seasonal wildflowers and a thriving colony of prairie dogs. Be sure to whistle at them as you cruise by.

After 3 miles the trail spits you out near the Fox Hollow Golf Course. Take the road (Fox Hollow Lane) or the wide sidewalk, watching for errant golf balls, drunken cart drivers, and wandering golfers. Wave to the bronze golfers (literally so, as opposed to the sun-bronzed golfers all around you) on your left as you follow the service road up the creek. After a short bit (around 1,000 feet), turn right (the sign says Bicycles and Service Vehicles Only) and start climbing. You're headed up the northeast face of the Bear Creek Dam. There's water for golfers toward the top of the climb near a sand bunker. Grab some if you're desperate. Enter the park proper at the top of the dam and follow the park road on a fast descent toward Bear Creek Lake. A right, a left, and a right will bring you to the entrance to the park at the northwest corner, near the intersection of Morrison Road and C-470. Pause here to reconnoiter. Decide if you want to ride up through Red Rocks or take the slightly easier C-470 Trail. To access the trail, ride .25 mile west on the trail leaving the park. Cross busy Morrison Road at the intersection and head north on Rooney Road. The C-470 Trail starts a few hundred feet up Rooney. To ride into Red Rocks, continue west on the trail, keeping Bear Creek to your left.

You'll soon come to the town of Morrison, notable for brunching weekend crowds and beer-drinking motorcycle heads, and a convenient place to grab a coffee or snack. When you're ready, leave the path and ride west along Morrison Road about .5 mile to Entrance #3 to Red Rocks. The gentle climb out of Morrison suddenly turns vicious. Turn right on the park road, then left onto Ship Rock Road, and climb up, up, up to the Upper South Parking Lot. This will connect to Trading Post Road (turn left) and in turn to Alameda Parkway (go right). A slightly easier ascent ignores Ship Rock Road and continues on Red Rocks Park Road to join Trading Post (a left). Even on concert days you're free to cycle in and out of the park with only a slight risk of running into a mushroom-buzzed Phish fan. As you suffer through the climb, distract yourself by trying to guess which of the many is Ship Rock.

From your high point in the park, make a fast descent on marginal pavement to Red Rocks Entrance #1 on Alameda Parkway. Go straight across the highway (Hogback Road), staying on the parkway. This next stretch through Dinosaur Ridge to Rooney on the east is closed to auto traffic, which makes it one of the nicer parts of the ride. Climb up through Dinosaur Ridge, famous for the 19th-century discovery of late-Jurassic-era dinosaurs. We're talking really big animals here, and there are a number of exhibits and panels scattered along both sides of the ridge. Some caution is required on the descent, since the visitors working their way up the east side

aren't necessarily expecting you to be descending at 35 mph. From here, go left on Rooney or rejoin the C-470 Trail just east of C-470. Turn right from Alameda to access the C-470 Trail. William F. Hayden Green Mountain Park is on your right, the Hogback on your left, and a dirt bike park in between. Climb up to and then under I-70, then descend to Colfax Avenue on Rooney. At Colfax turn right, then immediately left after 100 feet (alternatively, cross with the light and jump on the sidewalk), and follow the Golden Bike Path in a northerly direction, riding along next to C-470 until it crosses 6th Avenue (at a light). The path narrows but roughly follows Johnson Road to its intersection with 10th Avenue. On a low traffic day, riding right down Johnson is a great alternative.

At 10th, go east to McIntyre Street (it's one way against you, but there's a designated bike lane), north to Golden Road, then work your way through or around the small shopping center, using the Golden Triangle map and the Lookout Mountain Loop for detailed instructions. Once past the shopping center, you have a long and fast cruise back to Denver on 20th Avenue. The skyline views coming into the city are beautiful. Eastbound, there's a bike lane (or an adequate width) the length of 20th, save for one steep stretch between Willow Lane and Union Drive where the road narrows, drops precipitously, then climbs vertically 100 feet up the other side of Lena Gulch. In its infinite wisdom, the city has replaced the bike lane with what are euphemistically called "traffic calming" medians, theoretically designed to horizontally deflect traffic and slow the cars coming down both steep sides of Lena Gulch. For cyclists, there's nothing calm about this stretch. Instead, it forces us to duel mano a mano with the cars in a narrow band of road at high speed (going down) or ultra-slow speed (going up the other side). This is a good place to assert your right to the entire lane. Just before you come to Sloan's Lake, turn right on Depew Street and go south to 17th Avenue, then continue east. Seventeenth will bring you directly back to Invesco Field. Go either way around it. Finish the ride as you need to, along the Platte River or Cherry Creek trails.

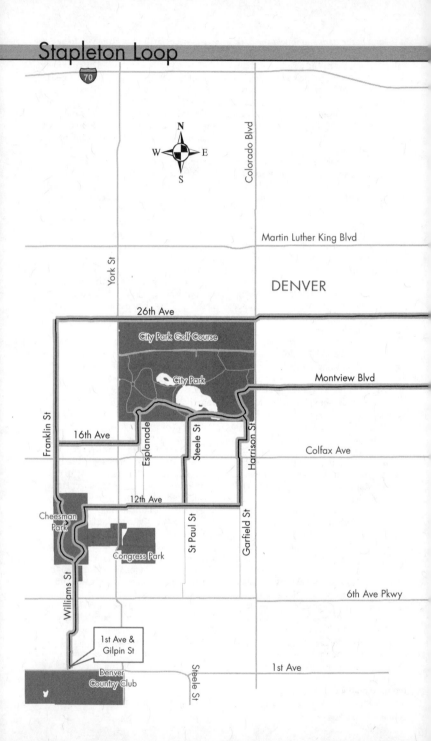

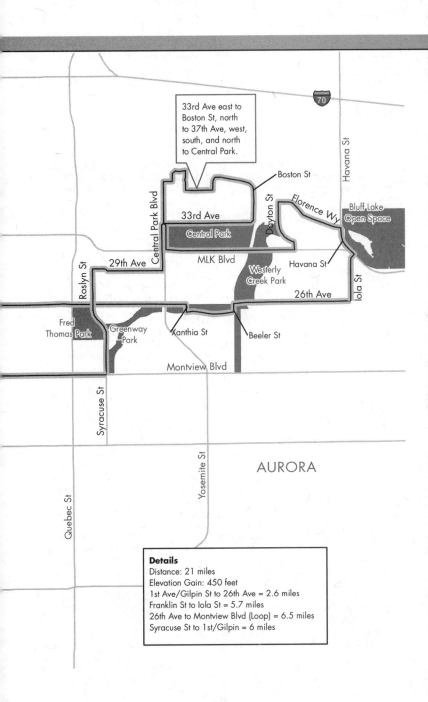

33rd Ave east to Boston St, north to 37th Ave, west, south, and north to Central Park.

Boston St

Havana St

Florence Wy

Bluff Lake Open Space

Central Park Blvd

Dayton St

33rd Ave

Central Park

MLK Blvd

Havana St

Roslyn St

29th Ave

Westerly Creek Park

Iola St

26th Ave

Fred Thomas Park

Greenway Park

Xanthia St

Beeler St

Montview Blvd

Syracuse St

Yosemite St

AURORA

Quebec St

Details
Distance: 21 miles
Elevation Gain: 450 feet
1st Ave/Gilpin St to 26th Ave = 2.6 miles
Franklin St to Iola St = 5.7 miles
26th Ave to Montview Blvd (Loop) = 6.5 miles
Syracuse St to 1st/Gilpin = 6 miles

Stapleton Loop

Distance: 21 miles
Elevation gain: 450 feet
Location: Northeast
Surface: 95% streets
Route finding: Easy
Traffic: Light. Crowded between Colfax and 26th Aves.
Direction: Both

Before Stapleton was a housing development and burgeoning Denver neighborhood, and before we had a monstrous bureaucracy called TSA, it was often possible to drive from central Denver to Stapleton airport, check your bags, and make it to your gate all in a little less than one hour. Now you can head out to Stapleton on your bicycle and explore one of the coolest new neighborhoods in Denver.

Stapleton began life as Denver Municipal Airport in 1929, survived the Great Depression, and expanded in 1944. Renamed for former Denver mayor Benjamin Stapleton, who'd championed the original airport, it eventually encompassed six runways and five terminals. Stapleton was decommissioned and the present Denver International Airport opened on February 27, 1995, in an elaborate pas de deux that required massive convoys of rental cars, baggage cars, and buses from Stapleton to DIA. When decommissioned, the old Stapleton airport covered almost 5,000 acres with a set of north-south runways that extended over and north of I-70.

In 1990, the Stapleton Foundation began planning to redevelop the site. Its master development plan called for mixed use, emphasizing, among other things, sustainability and environmental responsibility. Construction began in 2001, and the first residents arrived in 2004. Roughly 30 percent of the area is dedicated to parks and open space. Stapleton features a mix of housing types and styles, and there's a refreshing de-emphasis on the automobile. For example, no curb cuts are allowed on the street side of houses, and there's a strong emphasis on public and alternative transportation modes, which translates into wide streets, dedicated bike lanes, and superb cycling opportunities.

The route outlined and mapped here barely scratches the surface of what Stapleton offers. In addition to the streets, there are miles of trails that wander along Central, Greenway, and Westerly Creek parks, and they'll eventually join up with the Sand Creek Greenway. In the meantime, construction continues apace along the fringes of the neighborhood. In time, some of the routes may be slightly different than shown and described here. The goal of the Stapleton Loop, however, is to ride through and around Stapleton, taking in as many of the 35 housing styles and 24 parks as you can.

Begin at 1st Avenue and Gilpin Street, at the entrance to the Denver Country Club. Go north along Gilpin to 4th Avenue, jog east a half block to Williams Street, and continue north on Williams. Crossing 6th and 8th avenues, work your way up under the graceful trees to Cheesman Park (where someday autos may be restricted or forbidden). Exit Cheesman in the northwest corner on Franklin and keep going north to reach 26th Avenue. This will certainly be the slowest stretch of the ride as you make your way across Colfax Avenue and through the hospital district between 18th and 21st avenues. At 26th, go east. Things get better immediately once you cross York Street, where you have an unimpeded run to Colorado Boulevard, riding next to the City Park Golf Course. Pass through the Park Hill neighborhood. Enter Stapleton at Roslyn Street and continue east on 26th until you're forced south 1 block at Xanthia. This slight detour puts you on the south side of Greenway Park, en route to cross Westerly Creek Park. Return to 26th at Beeler Street.

Currently, Iola Street is as far east as you can go, but plans call for eventual development almost out to Peoria. Go north on Iola, then bear right to the light at Havana Street. Turn left on this major street and pedal quickly to Florence Way. Turn left. Florence becomes 35th Avenue, then turns south at Westerly Creek on Dayton Street. Future plans suggest that you'll eventually be able to ride straight west on 35th into the Central Park neighborhood, but for now go south on Dayton to MLK Jr. Boulevard and turn right. This major street never seems overly busy

and will carry you safely to Central Park Boulevard, about 1 mile. Turn north. On your left is the old airport's control tower, kept as a marker of the past. Continue to trace the outline of the neighborhood east along 33rd, north on Boston, and west on any combination of 35th to 37th avenues that works for you, then south again on Central Park. Ride south to 29th Avenue. Go right (west) and admire the mix of architectural styles here: the north side is determinedly modern and the south a sort of faux federal. If you hanker for coffee, stop in at Udi's for a pick-me-up, otherwise circle the roundabout and ride south on Roslyn all the way back down to Montview, your straight-line ticket back to City Park.

Consider exiting the park at Harrison or Steele Street, especially on a slow traffic day, jogging east to Garfield and St. Paul streets, respectively. With either exit, go south to 12th Avenue, then west through the interesting commercial strip of the Congress Park neighborhood. This stretch features cafés, small shops, and businesses and makes for a pleasant ride back to Cheesman Park. Exit Cheesman at Williams and head south to return to Speer and Gilpin.

Supplemental Maps

Cheesman Park Pavillion.

Confusion at the Confluence

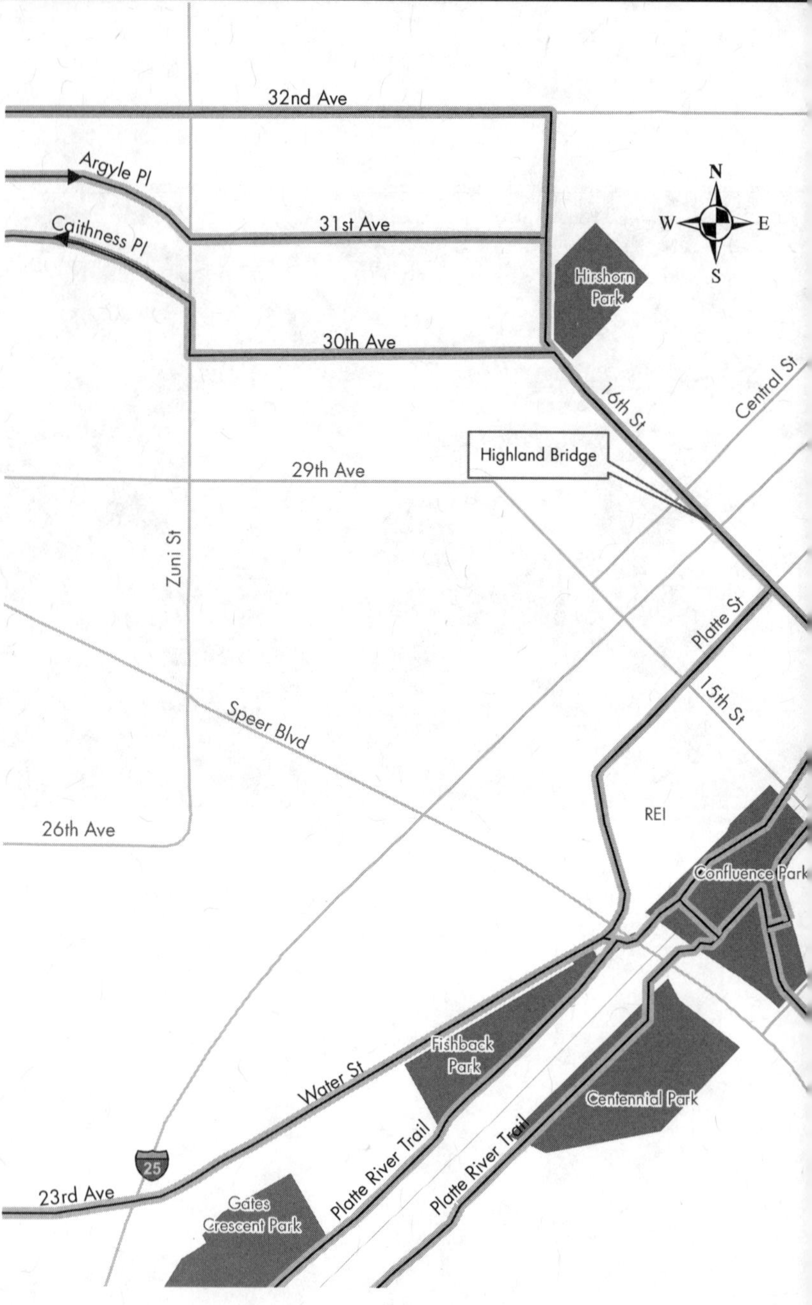

32nd Ave

Argyle Pl

Caithness Pl

31st Ave

30th Ave

Hirshorn Park

16th St

Central St

N
W   E
S

29th Ave

Highland Bridge

Zuni St

Platte St

Speer Blvd

15th St

26th Ave

REI

Confluence Park

Water St

Fishback Park

Centennial Park

23rd Ave

25

Gates Crescent Park

Platte River Trail

Platte River Trail

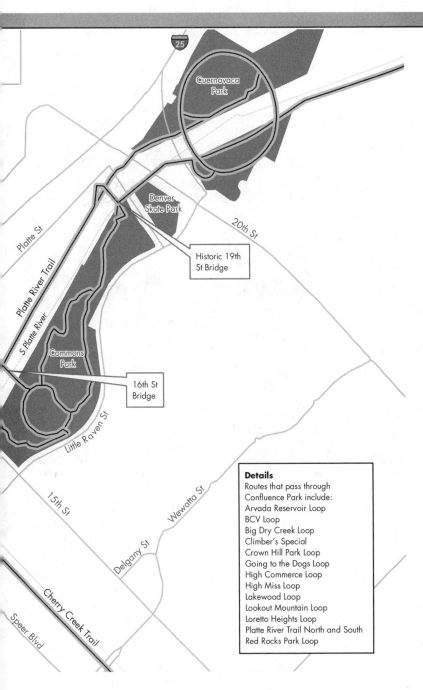

Details
Routes that pass through
Confluence Park include:
Arvada Reservoir Loop
BCV Loop
Big Dry Creek Loop
Climber's Special
Crown Hill Park Loop
Going to the Dogs Loop
High Commerce Loop
High Miss Loop
Lakewood Loop
Lookout Mountain Loop
Loretto Heights Loop
Platte River Trail North and South
Red Rocks Park Loop

Confusion at the Confluence

Distance: Negligible
Elevation gain: None
Surface: Varied: pavement, concrete, and dirt
Route finding: Advanced
Traffic: Heavy—mostly pedestrian, stroller, canine, cycle, and scooter
Direction: Both

Confluence Park, where the Platte River and Cherry Creek meet, has an interesting recent history. In the 1970s, then mayor Bill McNichols appointed a committee and charged it to reclaim and banks. In the ensuing years, Greenway has supported multiple projects up and down the Platte and far out into Douglas County along the Cherry Creek corridor. Successes include the bike path along 11 miles of the South Platte, the removal of multiple low-head dams along the river, and construction of at least 10 green spaces and parks on what were once landfills and dump sites. More recently, a nasty Xcel Energy substation was relocated and the ground reclaimed on the north part of the park, a great success in making the entire area people-friendly.

Pedestrian bridge at Confluence Park.

restore the South Platte River in Denver. McNichols gave the group $2 million in one-time funding and wished it well. Over the years the committee morphed into the Greenway Foundation, a non-profit organization that has become the watchdog and champion of the river ever since. Confluence Park, as it mostly exists today, was one of four original projects spearheaded by the foundation. It was designed and completed in 1975, long before anyone could predict the explosive growth in recreation along the river's

But, alas, we are still stuck with the awkward original design of Confluence Park. Nearly everything about it is wrong: the paths and bridge are too narrow, the down ramps are nearly impossible to navigate on a bicycle, and the rapids formed by artificial drops in the river are too close together. But who knew then what a great success it would be? All these will eventually be fixed, and there's even some hope that the disgracefully bad water that flows into the park from both directions will improve.

For cyclists, aside from the tight spaces and crowds (this isn't a place to pass people, but it might be a place to make passes at people), once you arrive at the park, the chief difficulty is in navigating from the park north to 19th Street. Going south is a snap: stay on the east bank and pedal upriver to the bridge at Invesco Field. To go the other direction, north, is a real piece of work. Frankly, it would be simpler to load your bicycle on a ferry and drift downstream to 19th Street than it is to twist and turn along the path. But since that's not an option, there are a few tricks to getting through.

The first difficulty lies in getting across 15th Street once you've crossed the Platte and are on the west bank (river is on your left as you face downstream). Here are your options.

1. Cross the river, go south and west to the small parking lot, and exit to go north on Water Street, then Platte Street. Cross 15th at the light with traffic. From there, proceed north to 16th or 19th streets (using the old bridge) to rejoin the path on the left and right side of the river, respectively.
2. Take a deep breath and slowly work your way down the original path on the west side of the river. It zigs and zags sharply down the narrow walkway. Two skilled and confident riders can pass each other in opposite directions, but most cyclists are probably better off walking.
3. Cross the river, then stay on the red cobblestone section just east of REI, and cross 15th Street at street grade. This works tolerably well under light traffic conditions but can be difficult at rush hour. It's made more complicated by the sharp curbs, uneven surfaces, and a small dirt ramp you must negotiate.

The second difficulty lies in getting back to the east bank after crossing 15th. The trail continues north on the west bank until it terminates somewhere north of 20th Street in a confusing crop circle of concrete. The trick is to get to the right side of the river before it ends in the concrete crop circle. Here are your options.

1. From Platte, go right at 16th, and cross the river on one of Denver's fabulous suspension bridges. Wind your way north through Commons Park to join the main trail on the east bank at 19th.
2. Travel north on the trail to 19th, then angle left and up to the historic 19th Street Bridge, cross the river, and immediately rejoin the main path on the river-right side of the Platte.
3. Finally, if you end up by mistake in the concrete crop circle, don't despair. Two small footbridges span the river between 20th and the railroad tracks. The south bridge (with its concrete ramp) is a slightly better option, only because the down ramp from the north bridge is dirt and gravel.

Don't let any of this discourage you from riding through or around the confluence. Whatever your preferred route, you'll quickly master it and forget that you were ever confused. Two comprehensive planning processes were under way in 2009 for both the River North and River South sections of the Platte, both at the urging and with the leadership of the Greenway Foundation. Perhaps in the next five years we'll have a new configuration that can accommodate all of us.

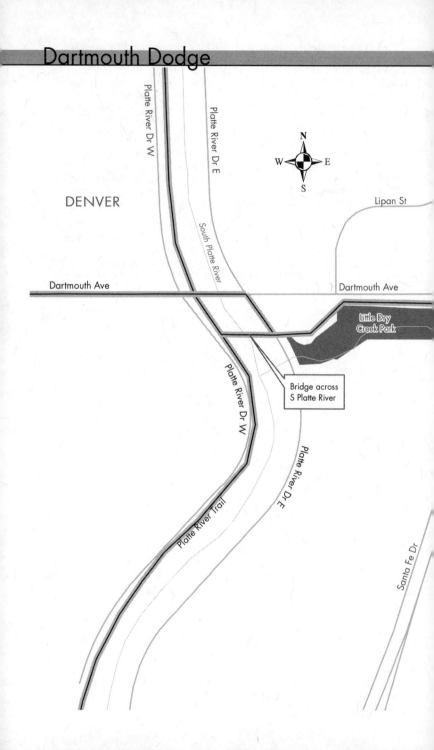

Platte River Dr W

Platte River Dr E

N
W · E
S

DENVER

Lipan St

South Platte River

Dartmouth Ave

Dartmouth Ave

Little Dry
Creek Park

Platte River Dr W

Bridge across
S Platte River

Platte River Dr E

Platte River Trail

Santa Fe Dr

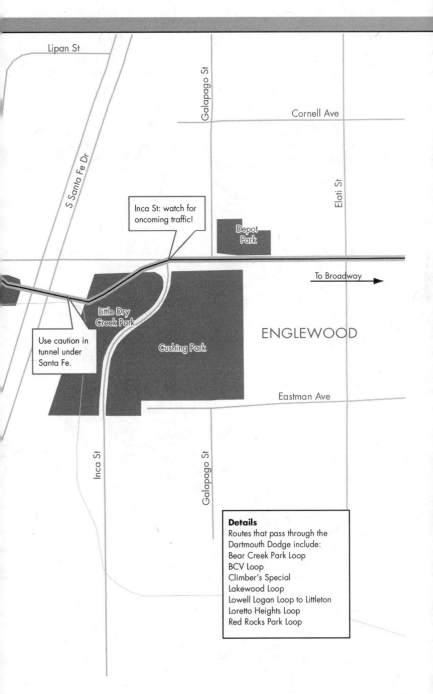

Lipan St

Galapago St

Cornell Ave

S Santa Fe Dr

Elati St

Inca St: watch for oncoming traffic!

Depot Park

To Broadway →

Little Dry Creek Park

ENGLEWOOD

Use caution in tunnel under Santa Fe.

Cushing Park

Eastman Ave

Inca St

Galapago St

Details
Routes that pass through the Dartmouth Dodge include:
Bear Creek Park Loop
BCV Loop
Climber's Special
Lakewood Loop
Lowell Logan Loop to Littleton
Loretto Heights Loop
Red Rocks Park Loop

Distance: N/A
Elevation gain: N/A
Surface: Concrete trail, tunnel, wooden bridge, pavement
Route finding: Easy
Traffic: Use caution when crossing Dartmouth Ave. and Platte River Dr.
Direction: N/A

The interchange at Dartmouth and Santa Fe Drive (a.k.a. US 85) is a pain for cyclists. Santa Fe has three through lanes in each direction, with double turn lanes from the north and south. The speed limit is 45 mph. People are in a hurry. Were that not enough, westbound Dartmouth traffic is squeezed from two lanes down to one, with the left-hand lane becoming a mandatory turn lane at Platte River Drive. To top it all off, the road inexplicably narrows from a reasonably wide street to one where it would be easy to get knocked off (your bicycle, I mean).

This doesn't mean you should never plow through the intersection (though you will usually have to wait for the light), but it does mean you should consider the alternatives. Enter the Dartmouth Dodge, thoughtfully provided as a storm-water enhancement to the Little Dry Creek system. Written directions are complicated by the fact that there are two Platte River drives, one on the west side of the river, one on the east.

- To go west on Dartmouth. Six blocks after the Broadway intersection, look for Depot (there's an old railroad depot there) and Cushing parks on your right and left. Move to the left lane. Just past Galapago Street, look left for Inca Street where it bisects the parks. Turn left to enter the trail at the southwest corner of Inca and Dartmouth. The trail winds under Santa Fe Drive and joins the east bank of Platte River Drive. Go north on Platte River, turn left on Dartmouth, and, once over the river, you'll be safely back on a decently wide two-lane road.
- From Dartmouth (westbound) to go north or south on the Platte River Trail, cross under Santa Fe as above. When you reach Platte River Drive, you'll see a bridge crossing the Platte. It connects to the Platte River Trail. Alternatively, if you're northbound and tolerant of industrial traffic and sometimes-rough roads, go north on Platte River Drive on the east bank. Cross Dartmouth at the light. The road winds north past the Littleton/Englewood Wastewater Treatment Plant and rejoins a spur of the Platte River Trail at Grant-Frontier Park, a little-used and shady place to stop for a drink of water and a snack. Grant-Frontier Park marks the site of one of the first Anglo settlements along the South Platte.
- To go east on Dartmouth, cross the river, turn right on Platte River Drive (the eastern version of it), ride south 200 feet, then turn left onto the cement path to wind your way back under Santa Fe to rejoin Dartmouth at Inca.
- From Dartmouth (eastbound) to go north on the Platte River Trail, simply turn left onto Platte River Drive (the western version of it) before you cross the river. Pick up the Platte River Trail 150 feet to the north.
- From the Platte River Trail (north or south) to go east or west on Dartmouth, use the exit ramps from the Platte River Trail. Exit on the north side of Dartmouth to go west, and the south side to go east.

Santa Fe Drive and Dartmouth Avenue, looking west.

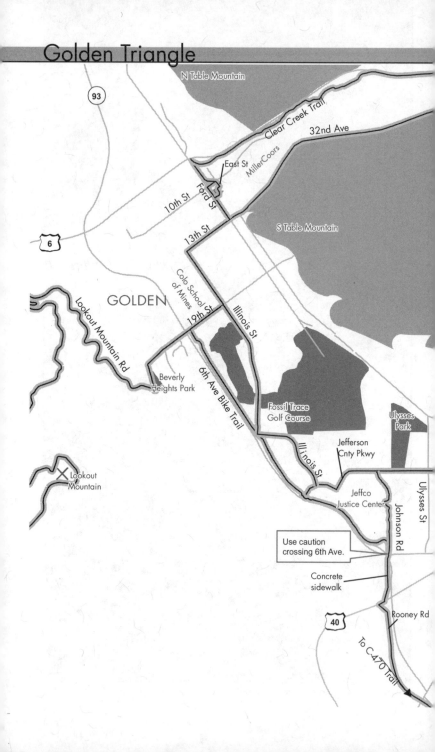

N Table Mountain

93

Clear Creek Trail

32nd Ave

East St

MillerCoors

10th St

Ford St

13th St

S Table Mountain

6

Colo School
of Mines

GOLDEN

19th St

Illinois St

Lookout Mountain Rd

Beverly
Heights Park

6th Ave Bike Trail

Fossil Trace
Golf Course

Ulysses
Park

Lookout
Mountain

Illinois St

Jefferson
Cnty Pkwy

Ulysses St

Jeffco
Justice Center

Johnson Rd

Use caution
crossing 6th Ave.

Concrete
sidewalk

40

Rooney Rd

To C-470 Trail

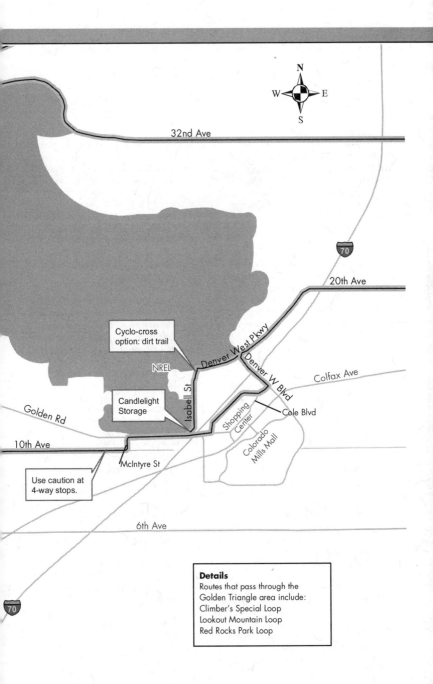

N
W E
S

32nd Ave

I-70

20th Ave

Cyclo-cross
option: dirt trail

Denver West Pkwy

Denver W Blvd

Colfax Ave

NREL

Isabell St

Candlelight
Storage

Shopping
Center

Cole Blvd

Golden Rd

Colorado
Mills Mall

10th Ave

McIntyre St

Use caution at
4-way stops.

6th Ave

I-70

Details
Routes that pass through the
Golden Triangle area include:
Climber's Special Loop
Lookout Mountain Loop
Red Rocks Park Loop

Distance: N/A
Elevation gain: N/A
Surface: Concrete trails, paved streets, and one short stretch of dirt trail "
Route finding: Advanced but interesting
Traffic: Heaviest along 32nd Ave., Denver West Pkwy. and Blvd., and Golden Rd.
Direction: N/A

On my first few attempts to get to and through Golden without riding on 32nd Avenue, I floundered a lot. But once I figured out a few tricks and shortcuts, it was a snap. Here's how to do it, with directions from Denver, from the north, to Lookout Mountain, and through Golden.

- From 20th Avenue (the cyclo-cross option), follow Denver West Parkway as it bends southwest. Cross Denver West Boulevard and ride toward the National Renewable Energy Lab. Just before the NREL sign, look for the pedestrian crossing. Go left. A short, steep dirt path drops down through a chain-link fence and rides along the edge of a small irrigation ditch for 100 feet. The path joins Isabell Street, which in turn joins Golden Road at Candlelight Storage, famous for its giant lighthouse. Go west on Golden Road for .4 mile to McIntyre Street. Go left on McIntyre and right on 10th Avenue.
- From 20th Avenue (through Denver West Village Shopping Center), follow Denver West Parkway as it bends southwest. Turn left on Denver West Boulevard and cross I-70. Turn right on Cole Boulevard into the shopping center and follow the shopping center road to Golden Road. Go right, under I-70, and ride to McIntyre Street. (You can avoid much of the traffic confusion in the shopping center by ducking behind the center just after turning right onto Cole. Look for the second right and zip through the parking lot to the quieter back side of the center. Return to Golden Road at the Outback Steakhouse. Go right to find McIntyre.)

- To ride to Lookout Mountain from Golden Road, turn left on McIntyre and immediately right on 10th Avenue. Follow 10th. It winds to Jefferson County Parkway near the justice center and sheriff's department. Turn right on Jeffco Parkway and right again in 1 block to Illinois Street. Illinois leads to the Fossil Trace Golf Course and dead-ends, so look for a spur of the 6th Avenue Trail to your left, just past the dirt road. Follow the spur out to 6th Avenue, go right, and then leave GBT again to regain Illinois. Ride it to 19th Avenue. Turn left to start climbing. If you miss the turn to Illinois or back from GBT, don't sweat it. The trail parallels 6th Avenue to 19th Street. At the light, cross 19th, reorient yourself, and start climbing.
- To reach the C-470 Trail, Rooney Road, and Red Rocks area, turn left from 10th Avenue at Johnson Road. Johnson appears after you cross Ulysses Street, climb a steep hill past Ulysses Park, and drop down the west side of the hill. Turn left at the stoplight. Going uphill on Johnson, you may want to use the broad sidewalk. From the south, coming downhill, I like the road. At 6th Avenue, use the crosswalk. If you've come up on the sidewalk it makes a disconcerting jog to the west just before the light, but don't get confused and mistakenly head out along 6th to Lookout Mountain. After crossing 6th, stay on the sidewalk/trail as it runs alongside C-470. At Colfax, go right, then left at the light (Rooney Road). Ride slightly more than 1 mile up Rooney to access the C-470 Trail on your left.
- To reach central Golden and the Clear Creek Trail, which runs 18 miles from Golden to the confluence of Clear Creek and the South Platte River in Adams County, follow the directions to Lookout Mountain. Cross 19th Street on Illinois Street and take it through the School of Mines, home to old trees, red brick buildings, and

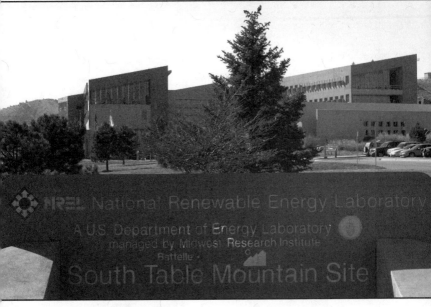

earnest engineering students. Keep going to 13th Street. Go right for 5 blocks, then left on Ford Street. Stop on the bridge at Clear Creek for a drink, to admire the river, or to read some of the (slightly) hokey stories the city has published on bronze tablets at the bridge. Take some time here, if you've got it, to wander up to the white-water park (north bank) or out onto Washington Street, 2 blocks west, to soak up some of Golden's down-home atmosphere before heading out Clear Creek for the fast ride home.

- The entrance to Clear Creek Trail is not marked or signed very well, and each time I come through this way I find myself a little surprised that it's so hard to find. Recently, I discovered that someone had conveniently pointed the way with chalk arrows on the sidewalk (but no words). Here's what to do. Cross Clear Creek on Ford. Turn right on 10th Street. Just before East Street, the next intersection, look for the trail on the north side of the street. Get on it

and go, but carefully at first. It runs uphill next to a moss-covered concrete channel for 100 yards before sharply switchbacking to the south and east. Alternatively, you can take the bed of the creek just downstream from Ford to cut through the small park (Vanover). A bridge and a short piece of trail will lead you to East Street. Go left (north) to find the Clear Creek Trail.

Highlands Lowdown

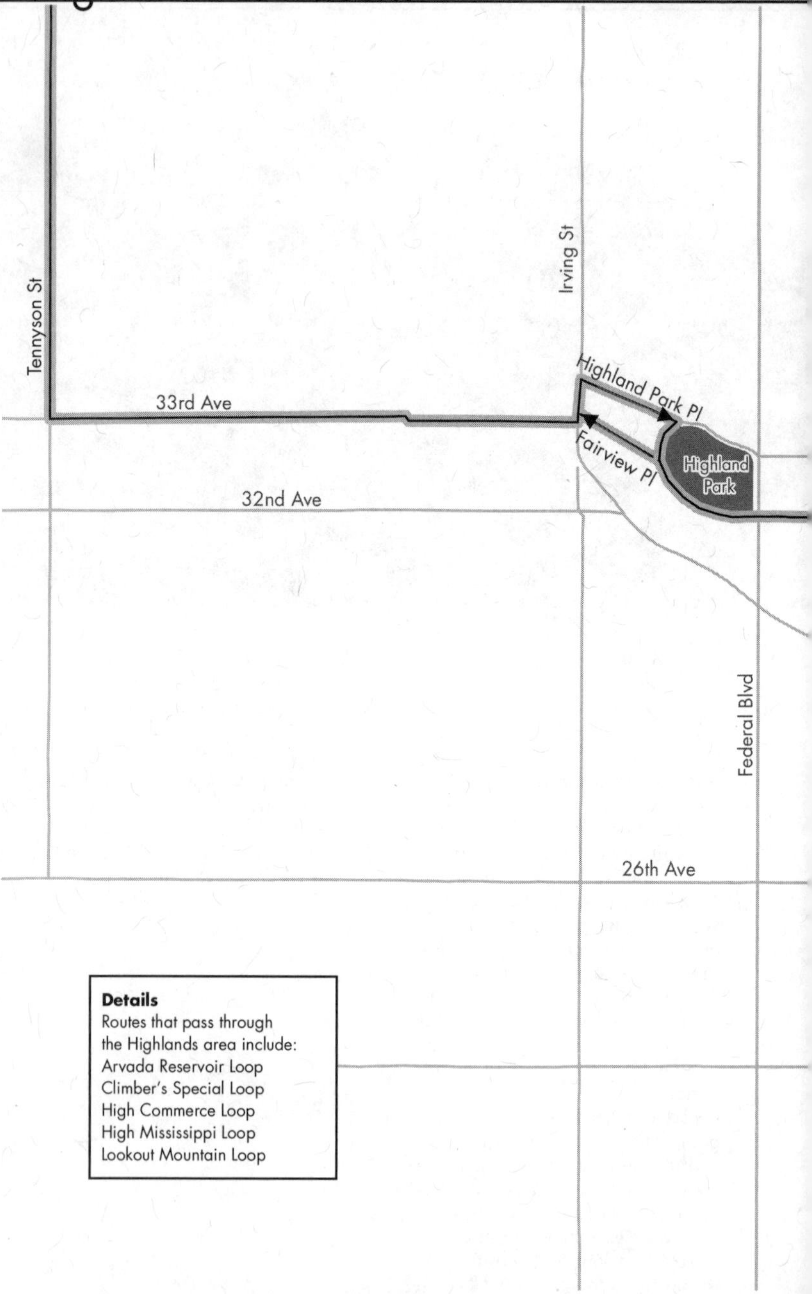

Tennyson St
Irving St
Highland Park Pl
33rd Ave
Fairview Pl
Highland Park
32nd Ave
Federal Blvd
26th Ave

Details
Routes that pass through the Highlands area include:
Arvada Reservoir Loop
Climber's Special Loop
High Commerce Loop
High Mississippi Loop
Lookout Mountain Loop

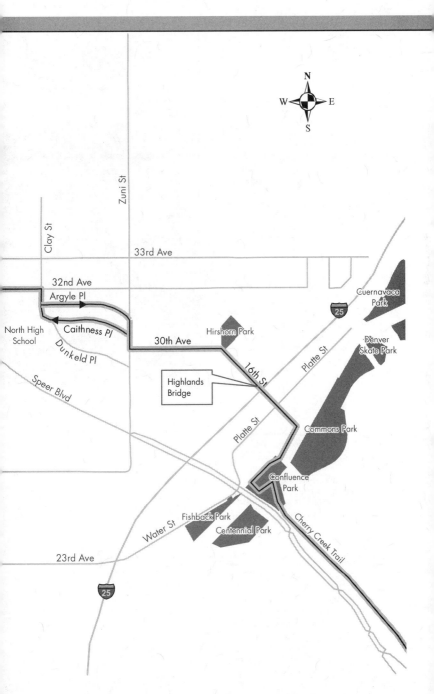

North High
School

Clay St

Zuni St

33rd Ave

32nd Ave

Argyle Pl

Caithness Pl

Dunkeld Pl

Speer Blvd

30th Ave

Highlands
Bridge

16th St

Hirshorn Park

Cuernavaca
Park

Denver
Skate Park

Platte St

Commons Park

Platte St

Confluence
Park

Water St

Fishback Park

Centennial Park

Cherry Creek Trail

23rd Ave

Highlands Lowdown

Distance: N/A
Elevation gain: N/A
Surface: All streets
Route finding: Moderate but challenging
Traffic: Moderate
Direction: N/A

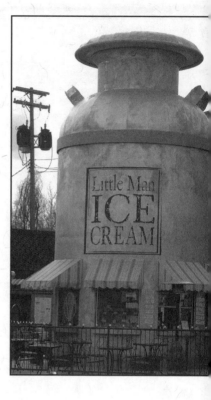

There are many great ways to get through the Highlands area, and it would be worth your while to spend some time just wandering about on your bicycle to appreciate the history and richness of the area. Lowell, Irving, Tejon, 29th, and 26th barely scratch the surface. Farther north, north of 38th Avenue, the Sunnyside area between Federal Boulevard and Pecos Street is also worth a short tour. For now, however, we're just concerned with getting from Confluence Park to Tennyson Street, a key link in several of the rides in this guide.

Start at Confluence Park and make your way to 16th Street on Water and Platte streets via the Platte River Trail, or using the bridge from Commons Park. Cross I-25 on the new Highland Bridge and climb up to 30th Avenue. Look for the red organic sculpture (*National Velvet*) by local artist John McEnroe on the east end of the bridge. Go left on 30th to Zuni, then right a short .5 block. Go left into the old Scottish Highlands neighborhood on Caithness Place (one way). A right on Clay Street and an immediate left on 32nd Avenue bring you past North High School and to a light at which you will cross Federal Boulevard. Once across Federal, swing partway around Highland Park, then go diagonally left to Fairview Place (one way) for 1 short block. At its end, go left to 33rd Avenue and on out to Tennyson. Thirty-third is a great alternative to 32nd: there are fewer cars and slower traffic on a tree-shaded residential street.

If you return through the Highlands on 33rd, you must adjust for the one-way streets. At Irving, go north 1 block to Highland Park Place, then right to swing around Highland Park. Ride 32nd east to Clay Street, go right, and take an immediate left on Argyle Place, the one-way eastbound twin of Caithness. At Zuni, go right to 30th Avenue, then left on 30th to return to 16th Street and the South Platte River.

Mississippi Muddle

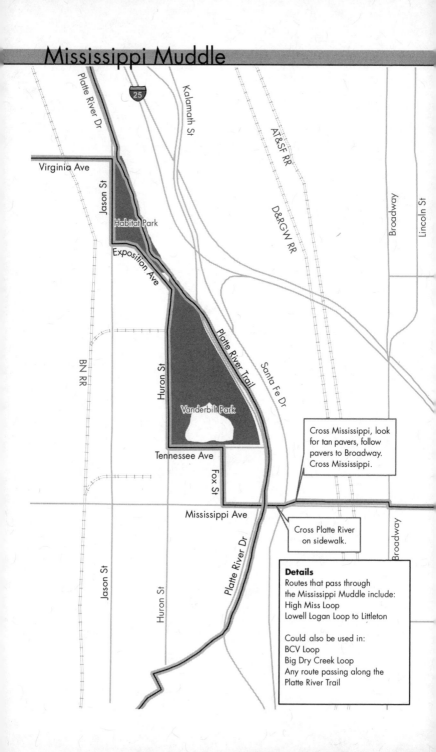

I-25

Platte River Dr

Kalamath St

AT&SF RR

D&RGW RR

Broadway

Lincoln St

Virginia Ave

Jason St

Habitat Park

Exposition Ave

Huron St

BN RR

Platte River Trail

Santa Fe Dr

Vanderbilt Park

Tennessee Ave

Fox St

Mississippi Ave

Jason St

Huron St

Platte River Dr

Broadway

Cross Mississippi, look for tan pavers, follow pavers to Broadway. Cross Mississippi.

Cross Platte River on sidewalk.

Details
Routes that pass through the Mississippi Muddle include:
High Miss Loop
Lowell Logan Loop to Littleton

Could also be used in:
BCV Loop
Big Dry Creek Loop
Any route passing along the Platte River Trail

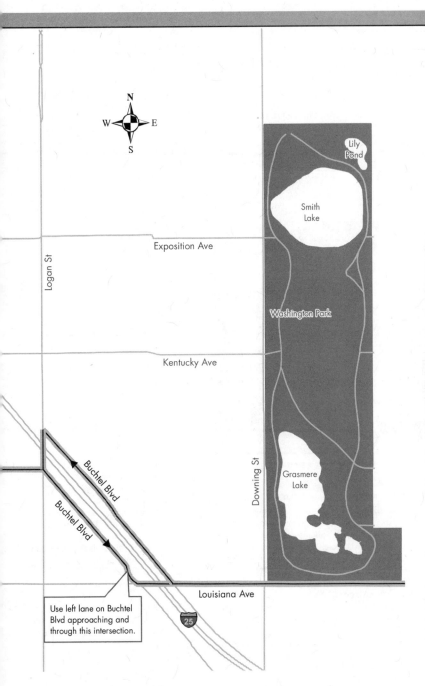

N
W   E
S

Logan St

Exposition Ave

Kentucky Ave

Downing St

Buchtel Blvd

Buchtel Blvd

Louisiana Ave

Use left lane on Buchtel
Blvd approaching and
through this intersection.

25

Lily Pond

Smith Lake

Washington Park

Grasmere Lake

Distance: N/A
Elevation gain: N/A
Surface: A mix of streets, trails, and sidewalks, depending on your mood and the traffic conditions
Route finding: Advanced
Traffic: Intense at times
Direction: Both

When Denver was developing into a city, the earliest settlers used the rivers and creeks of the area, and the land next to them, as pathways. Denver isn't unique in this, of course; settlers everywhere have done it. It makes sense. If a river has already cut a path through the mountains or along the plains, there will be game

Mississippi Avenue, looking west.

trails and native trails there already. Horse trails succeeded game trails. Wagon trails succeeded horse trails. Pretty soon there were railroads and automobiles, and suddenly, today, cyclists find themselves on the wrong side of the equivalent of the Berlin Wall. The South Platte River is a good case in point. Between Hampden Avenue and Confluence Park, there are precious few routes from west to east (and back) that don't require some ingenuity, if not strong urban-cycling skills. Dartmouth Avenue is very useful. Eighth and 13th avenues are sketchy but negotiable, though this will change in 2012

when the West light-rail line is opened. But in the middle Platte region, things are tricky. The official bike map for the city has routes depicted at Iowa Avenue and Alameda, but neither is very cycle-friendly. The Alameda route takes you on a sketchy sidewalk, and the Iowa route leads you down a one-lane underpass trafficked primarily, as far as I can tell, by irritable truck drivers with deadlines to beat.

Shown here is a safe west-to-east route across Santa Fe, the South Platte, and under the railroad tracks. The route takes you off the streets and onto the sidewalk, but if you're a determined urban cyclist, you'll want to tackle Mississippi head on. Directions are included for that, too.

- For the sidewalk route, begin at the traffic light on Mississippi and Platte River Drive. When you get a green light, head to the sidewalk to let the traffic behind you get past. Cross Santa Fe to the sidewalk on the east side. Wait for the light to change. Then cross northbound to a median with tan pavers. Cross no farther. Go east on the pavers and follow them to a sidewalk that takes you safely under the tracks and to the northwest corner of Broadway and Mississippi. When you come to Broadway, either cross south to Mississippi or east to Broadway and carry on. Return to eastbound Mississippi from here.
- For the urban cycling route, cross Platte River Drive and get on the sidewalk if there are cars breathing down your neck. As you slow-pedal across the Platte, let the cars pass you by. Keep going across Santa Fe and rejoin the fray eastbound on Mississippi. There are two lanes so there's room for cars to pass if they come up behind you as you ride from Santa Fe to Broadway. It's a fun sprint. Significant development is under way here. The old Gates Rubber Company has been largely remediated and plans are afoot for a mixed-use development on the 105 acres. As those plans develop, access to and from the west should improve.

Acknowledgments

Much that is good about this book I owe to others. Michael Henry first put the idea of a guidebook in my head the day (a long way outside Montrose) I forgot my cycling shoes. He has been, along with Andrea Dupree and the rest of the Lighthouse Writers crowd, a tremendous source of wisdom and inspiration for almost a decade. Shari Caudron and Bill Henderson and the writers from the Writer's Block gave me welcome space in which to write. My father, who at 87 continues to cycle, has been a great source of inspiration. My brother, Chad, loaned me my first real road bike many years ago. Matt Hupperts from The Bicycle Doctor kept me in tubes and kept my bike in tune.

Several people tried out or suffered through early versions of some of these rides, and I'm grateful for their companionship and feedback: Jim Angell, Chris Crawford, Adam Eichberg, David Korman, Jay McCormick, and David Readerman. Emily Sinclair deserves special mention both for putting up with me getting us lost and for her tolerance for the many long absences this book entailed.

I have also been lucky to meet many other riders along the way, all of whose names I have since forgotten, but all of whom passed a few miles with me, gave me air or a tube when I needed it, or otherwise pointed me in the right direction. I am deeply indebted to them.

Other writers and riders have gone before me on some of these rides, including Kurt Magsamen (*Cycling Colorado's Mountain Passes*, Golden, CO: Fulcrum, 2002); Michael Seeberg (*Road Biking Colorado*, Englewood, CO: Westcliffe, 2003), and Robert Hurst (*Road Biking Colorado's Front Range*, Guilford, CT: Falcon, 2005). Bob Prehn has a treasure trove of local maps and information on his website, www.geobiking.org, and John Klever's maps and construction/detour/flood updates are an extraordinary and invaluable resource for the community, at www.trailsdenver.com. For inspiration, geographic information system (GIS) data, and cartographic support, I am grateful to Steve Hick; the GIS departments of Adams, Arapahoe, and Douglas counties; and those of Denver, Lakewood, Golden, and Arvada. Beverly Haddon and Angie Malpiede graciously helped me understand Stapleton's development and transportation plans, and how the latter ties into Denver's master planning process. At the City of Denver, Diane Barrett pointed me in all the right directions, Mary Dulacki helped me access police department data on accidents involving bicycles, and Parry Burnap got me up to speed on the city's Bike Initiative and bike sharing program.

Finally, Faith Marcovecchio, Katie Wensuc, and Jack Lenzo at Fulcrum gave this book its final shape and form; for their skillful help I will be ever in their debt. Any errors in the book, of course, are mine alone.

BikeDenver promotes and encourages bicycling as an energy-efficient, nonpolluting, healthy, and enjoyable transportation alternative within the City and County of Denver. www.BikeDenver.org, 1536 Wynkoop St., Ste. 801, Denver, CO 80202.

Denver Bike Sharing aims to change to transportation culture in Denver by implementing a public bike-sharing system call Denver B-cycle. Funded with grants, sponsorships, and transaction fees, Denver Bike Sharing launched the system in 2010 with 600 bikes and 40+ stations citywide. www.denverbikesharing.org.

Bicycle Colorado is a statewide nonprofit organization dedicated to building a bicycle-friendly Colorado. They advocate for more bike lanes and paths, better education and trails, and bicycle-friendly laws. The organization works primarily at the state and regional level, where so many of the policy decisions that affect bicyclists are made. www.bicyclecolo.org, 1525 Market St., Ste. 100, Denver, CO 80202.

The Rocky Mountain Cycling Club caters to active, enthusiastic cyclists of intermediate and advanced levels and interests and arranges club rides and events throughout the season ranging from 20 to over 200 miles. www.rmccrides.com.

The Denver Bicycle Touring Club promotes recreational and commuter cycling, bike safety, and education of the general public in cycling matters. It's active in advocacy and cycling planning with local governments and organizes and sponsors weekend and weekday rides. www.dbtc.org, P.O. Box 260517, Denver, CO 80226.

Colorado supports a robust amateur racing scene, with too many individual local clubs to list here. A good place to get started is with the American Cycling Association, www.americancycling.org, which sanctions most road and cyclo-cross racing in Colorado and southeast Wyoming. It maintains a list of local clubs on the website. Racing at the national level is managed by USA Cycling, www.usa.cycling.org. There's no single source for local and regional charity events and rides, but a good place to start is www.coloradobicyclerides.com, which maintains a good list.

Index of Rides by Length

Name	Miles	Elevation Gain	Location	Page
Cook Park Loop	17	500	Central	54
High Miss Loop	17	675	NW	74
Lowry Intervals	18	300	Central	96
Loretto Heights Loop	19	875	SW	88
B-C-V Loop	20	675	Central	18
Stapleton Loop	21	450	NE	112
Central Parks Trifecta	22	600	Central	30
The Colonel's Loop	20–23	600	NE	50
Going to the Dogs Loop	22–23	500	NE	66
Big Dry Creek Trail Loop	25	900	S	26
Platte River Trail North	25	250	NW	100
High Commerce Loop	26	725	NE	70
Cherry Creek–Heather Gardens Loop	22–27	750	SE	38
Cherry Creek Trail and Reservoir Loop	12–27	365–875	SE	42
Crown Hill Loop	18–27	825	NW	58
Lakewood Loop	27	1,075	W	78
Lowell–Logan Loop to Littleton	27	1,300	SW	92
Cherry Creek Anti-Trail Loop	32	1,200	SE	34
Platte River Trail South	32	225	SW	104
Dove Valley Loop	36–40	1,575	SE	62
Arvada Reservoir Loop	43	1,800	NW	14
Bear Creek Park Loop	44	1,800	SW	22
Red Rocks Park Loop	42	2,500	SW	108
Lookout Mountain Loop	46–52	2,600–3,300	W	82
Climber's Special	70	5,400	NW, W, and SW	46

Index of Rides by Elevation Gain

Name	Miles	Elevation Gain	Location	Page
Platte River Trail South	32	225	SW	104
Platte River Trail North	25	250	NW	100
Lowry Intervals	18	300	Central	96
Stapleton Loop	21	450	NE	112
Cook Park Loop	17	500	Central	54
Going to the Dogs Loop	22–23	500	NE	66
Central Parks Trifecta	22	600	Central	30
The Colonel's Loop	20–23	600	NE	50
High Miss Loop	17	675	NW	74
B-C-V Loop	20	675	Central	18
High Commerce Loop	26	725	NE	70
Cherry Creek–Heather Gardens Loop	22–27	750	SE	38
Crown Hill Loop	18–27	825	NW	58
Loretto Heights Loop	19	875	SW	88
Cherry Creek Trail and Reservoir Loop	12–27	365–875	SE	42
Big Dry Creek Trail Loop	25	900	S	26
Lakewood Loop	27	1,075	W	78
Cherry Creek Anti-Trail Loop	32	1,200	SE	34
Lowell–Logan Loop to Littleton	27	1,300	SW	92
Dove Valley Loop	36–40	1,575	SE	62
Arvada Reservoir Loop	43	1,800	NW	14
Bear Creek Park Loop	44	1,800	SW	22
Red Rocks Park Loop	42	2,500	SW	108
Lookout Mountain Loop	46–52	2,600–3,300	W	82
Climber's Special	70	5,400	NW, W, and SW	46

Index of Rides by Location

Name	Miles	Elevation Gain	Location	Page
Lowry Intervals	18	300	Central	96
Cook Park Loop	17	500	Central	54
Central Parks Trifecta	22	600	Central	30
B-C-V Loop	20	675	Central	18
Stapleton Loop	21	450	NE	112
Going to the Dogs Loop	22–23	500	NE	66
The Colonel's Loop	20–23	600	NE	50
High Commerce Loop	26	725	NE	70
Platte River Trail North	25	250	NW	100
High Miss Loop	17	675	NW	74
Crown Hill Loop	18–27	825	NW	58
Arvada Reservoir Loop	43	1,800	NW	14
Climber's Special	70	5,400	NW, W, and SW	46
Big Dry Creek Trail Loop	25	900	S	26
Cherry Creek–Heather Gardens Loop	22–27	750	SE	38
Cherry Creek Trail and Reservoir Loop	27	365–875	SE	42
Cherry Creek Anti-Trail Loop	32	1,200	SE	34
Dove Valley Loop	36–40	1,575	SE	62
Platte River Trail South	32	225	SW	104
Loretto Heights Loop	19	875	SW	88
Lowell–Logan Loop to Littleton	27	1,300	SW	92
Bear Creek Park Loop	44	1,800	SW	22
Red Rocks Park Loop	42	2,500	SW	108
Lakewood Loop	27	1,075	W	78
Lookout Mountain Loop	46–52	2,600–3,300	W	82